FOR MORE than a hur
Dundee has been divideu ...
loyalties. Today, "the great divide" is one
street—Tannadice Street—which separates
by some 300 yards the home grounds of
Dundee United and Dundee Football Clubs.

Jute made Dundee. At the beginning of
the nineteenth century the town was a small
port of some 30,000 people. One hundred
years later that figure had increased *more
than fivefold,* and by then more than 30,000
people worked in the Jute industry alone.
Dundee was therefore a city of immigrants
and a large proportion of them were of Irish
origin or ancestry, but the two "nations"
which grew up in the town were not Scots
and Irish or even Protestant and Catholic.
They were rich and poor. While jute made
vast fortunes for some who inhabited
mansions in the West End or Broughty
Ferry, it created squalor for virtually all
others who shared tenements which were
grim even by the standards of comparable
industrial towns. There was therefore a
desperate need for some kind of physical and
indeed spiritual diversion. To some extent
football provided this.

ACROSS THE GREAT DIVIDE looks at
the origins of both Dundee football clubs in
the dark days of the late nineteenth century.
It documents their early successes and
follows them through their years of
frustration and revival, culminating in
recent years first in Dundee's then United's
fantastic progress to the verge of European
greatness. But *ACROSS THE GREAT
DIVIDE* is more than another football book.
It is a story related against the background of
a changing world, with all the social and
economic implications involved. It is a book
that will appeal to the vast army of football
fans everywhere but also to a more general
public in that it throws new light on the city
of Dundee and its people. In that sense it is a
true social history.

ACROSS THE GREAT DIVIDE

Across The Great Divide

Jim Wilkie

MAINSTREAM
PUBLISHING

First published in 1984 by
MAINSTREAM PUBLISHING COMPANY (EDINBURGH) LTD.
7 Albany Street
Edinburgh EH1 3UG

The author wishes to express his thanks to Flora McNeill (Glasgow UIG) —
who typed above and beyond the call; The staff of the Dundee Library —
Local History Room; The staff of the Mitchell Library (Glasgow) — The
Glasgow Room; Kevin McCarra; Pat Woods; George Hill; Lochee Harp; D C
Thomson Photofiles; Donnie Coutts; The Scottish Football League (David
Thomson); The Scottish Football Association (Marjory Nimmo); and the
legendary Billy Kay.

The Book is Dedicated to: The Citizens of Dundee and my family, in and
around the town.
Love to Lorna..

ISBN 0 906391 76 8 (Cloth)
ISBN 0 906391 77 6 (Paperback)

Typeset in 11/13 point Garamond by Studioscope in conjunction with
Mainstream Publishing.
Printed by Forsyth Middleton & Co. Ltd., Kilsyth.

Illustrations

Introduction

IF YOU WERE to describe the City of Dundee, probably the last word which would come to mind is "beautiful". More than likely you would use adjectives like "grey", "grim", even "industrial" or "peculiar" — and Dundee certainly is an unusual city. For a start its history and dialect are unique — sub-cultural almost — but it's tucked away in an obscure corner of Scotland's east coast, by-passed almost invariably by those heading north to the "romantic" Scottish Highlands, or south to the "glittering" conurbations. And you'd never call Dundonians romantic. Hardened by centuries of economic and political uncertainty, their appearance and manner are often regarded as dour and uncompromising. Yet anyone who has spent any time actually living or working there knows that this is nothing like the whole story.

Dundee's splendid situation on the north bank of the Tay estuary can be seen to good advantage from Balgay Hill and if that view of the old town at the foot of the Law, linked to the green hills of Fife by two spectacular bridges, with the promontory of Broughty Ferry beyond, doesn't strike a chord, then you might as well carry on looking, either for your fortune, or your Granny's Hielan' Hame.

One way or another, when Dundee United Football Club won their first Scottish Premier League Championship in Season 1982-83, the city was described by one of the country's best football writers, Ian Archer, as "lonely, neglected and almost beleaguered". It was true. Dundee, like everywhere else in Britain, was trying to combat the worst economic conditions for fifty years; that very week the large workforce of the Timex Electronics Company was under siege by a Tory government for daring to strike on a point of principle when the unemployment rate stood locally at over 16%; and the red, black, white and green flag which hung in the City Chambers acknowledged the achievements not of their now famous footballing sons, but of the Palestine Liberation Organisation.

The city, of course, did pay handsome tribute to the club and players who brought such honour to it by winning the most keenly-fought and thrilling Premier League competition since its inception, and civic chests swelled with additional pride, for this relatively small club had secured its victory with a pool, generally speaking, of fourteen players, eight of whom came from the Tayside Region and seven from Dundee itself. Aberdeen FC, by comparison, with a city to themselves, oil-rich and booming, won the European Cup Winners' Cup some three days earlier with a pool of sixteen players, only four of whom could be regarded as locals.

And Dundee United certainly do *not* have their hometown to themselves. Literally across the street from their ground, Tannadice Park, in the north end of the inner city stands Dens Park, in some ways a more imposing stadium which, for many years after its construction as the home of Dundee Football Club, cast something of a shadow over Tannadice. For whilst their rivals languished in the old Scottish Second Division for the greater part of the first sixty years of their existence, Dundee FC won every major trophy in the Scottish game, had a substantial number of their players capped by Scotland, and reached a European Cup semi-final, in 1963.

As surely as the seasons change, however, so too do footballing fortunes, and the early 1980s saw Dundee United finally and conclusively emerge from that shadow as a leading club, not only in Scottish, but in European football. And these things are important. Why else, for example, would anyone remember Jock Stein, Bob Shankly or Jim McLean?

Jim Wilkie
October 1984

1

ALTHOUGH THERE are no records, it can be assumed that some kind of football has been part of man's life for thousands of years. Classical Egyptian, Greek and Chinese literature contain explicit references to the sport — in one exotic Chinese version, teams vied with one another to score goals by kicking the ball through an opening in a silken net — and the Romans, who are said to have fostered football as part of their military training, are generally assumed to have brought the game to Britain. Football probably belongs to the category of primitive fertility rites, with the ball representing the sun or the head of an animal sacrifice and, given that reliable references to the game occur only after 1066, some believe the Normans developed it from the rites of Roman saturnalia (a feast concerned with fertility).

The first extensive description of British football dates from the London of 1175. It is an account by one William Fitzstephen of how, on Shrove Tuesday that year, the youth of the city spent part of the day cockfighting "and in other boyish pursuits, and after dinner, they went to a local piece of ground . . . just outside the city for the famous game of ball". Soon, authorities came to view the game as a nuisance and, as in the case of other sports, a danger to national security on the grounds that it interfered with the country's defence, in which efficiency with bows and arrows was most essential. There were other grounds too on which the authorities based the opposition to football, for the *lack of any code* often caused the games to degenerate into riotous running battles, and this "mob" or "rough" football, as it was known, probably was not dissimilar to the famous "Ba game" which still persists in Kirkwall.

In 1314 King Edward II of England, following his humiliation at Bannockburn, where his archers were thought to have performed particularly badly, issued an edict forbidding football in his domain. Now, whereas it might be supposed the Scots would logically adopt the opposite viewpoint, and cultivate the warlike potential of their football, this proved not to be the case, and indeed, the game was also frowned upon by Scottish kings of the fifteenth century. In 1603, however, James VI of Scotland assumed the crown of a united Britain as James I ("the Wisest fool in Christendom"), and football was again recognised, and even encouraged. By then, of course, archery had become redundant with the introduction of firearms, and by the nineteenth century, the more refined and organised form of man's primitive kicking games was becoming popular everywhere. In this refinement and organisation, the educated classes played a prominent part.

In keeping with earlier aristocratic interest, "rough" football was played at the English public schools, and playing it was one of the ways in which senior boys dominated others. During the 1830s and 1840s, however, the public schools, like several other important institutions, underwent reform and with that reform went the reform of football. Also, many of the pupils wished to go on playing at University, and since different schools had different ideas as to how the game should be played, it was at Cambridge University, first in 1848 and then in the 1860s, that experiments finally produced a body of rules which appeared to have a fairly wide acceptance, first in England and then in Scotland, where Queen's Park Football Club was established in 1867, and the Scottish Cup instituted in 1873. Eight teams competed for that first cup — Queen's Park, Clydesdale, Vale of Leven, Dumbreck, Third Lanark Volunteer Reserves, Eastern, Granville and Kilmarnock — and they effectively thus formed the Scottish Football Association. This was followed by the formation of the Scottish League in 1890, and the first League Handbook of 1891-92 listed a First Division of twelve Clubs, an Alliance of twelve, a Federation of twelve, a Midland League of ten, an Ayrshire League of ten, and a Northern League of eight — three of whose members came from Dundee.

Dundee, in the late nineteenth century, was a textile town, with jute its most valuable commodity. Jute had come to Dundee for a variety of reasons: the uncertainty of flax supplies from territory controlled by

Russia, with whom Britain had recently been at war; jute's relative abundance and cheapness; the impact of exceptional demand as a result of the aforementioned war, and the cotton famine of the 1860s; local technical progress in engineering; the willingness of Victorians to plough back profits; and the almost universal economic boom in the 1870s; all these served to stimulate expansion.

In 1839 the industry did not exist; in 1890, out of a total workforce (i.e. those in employment) of 80,000, more than 40,000 worked in jute, nearly all of them in or around Dundee. Perhaps the most astonishing thing, however, is that at least 30,000 of those were women and children (female labour being thought cheaper and more pliable than its male equivalent) and the result was the development of a kind of "mill-girl culture" which would have touched most families in the town, and therefore been an important factor in the shaping of the Dundee character and way of life.

Textiles were not the only source of employment in the town, however. Shipbuilding and engineering were also major employers — although at this time printing and confectionery were not — and by the 1880s and 1890s, most working people had won the privilege of a Saturday half-day. Saturday afternoon, therefore, became a great time for "true" leisure (as opposed to the "enforced" leisure of unemployment) and a general interest in sports began to develop among the masses.

Initially, the geography of Dundee, with its steep, south-facing site, was not particularly suited to sport, although it was beginning to change, since flat land was sought-after, for industrial premises as well as for sports grounds, and both the Harbour Board and Town Council were beginning to reclaim land. Indeed, the reclamation of Riverside Park (or the "Cowp" as it is sometimes known) to the west of the Tay Bridge was begun at this time. It now, of course, also houses Dundee Airport.

There is no fixed date when football first began in Dundee. A game called "football" is first recorded as being played in the city in the early 1870s but this, as previously stated, was a time when Association Football was still in an experimental stage throughout Britain, and the (amateur) game which was played by the Dundee Clubs bore a greater resemblance to present-day rugby than football, with opposition coming from "good" schools and universities. Even at this, however,

11

there was still some confusion, as a letter to the editor of the *Dundee Advertiser* of 17 January 1873 illustrates:

> Sir,
>
> The report in Monday's *Advertiser* of the football match played at St Andrews between the University team and those of Dundee and Broughty is not altogether correct. The match was to have been twenty a side, but the North of Tay only succeeded in mustering 14 players.
>
> Four St Andrews men, however, were transferred to their side and the game was played eighteen a side. Your report should also have stated that an additional touch-down-behind goal was claimed by the St Andrews team.
>
> I am, etc,
> Joseph Brown,
> 72 North St, St Andrews.

In his footnote, a slightly-rattled Editor remarked that "It seems impossible to get reports of these matches to which objection is not taken by some of the players". How right he was.

Between 1874 and 1876 two Clubs, one called Dundee United and the other Dundee, had fixtures at Blackness Park and Baxter Park respectively, playing rugby rules. But many experiments were taking place locally now, and the following year an *Advertiser* report (13 March 1877) referred to one side's "splendid passing game which brought out the great superiority of the Association over the Rugby style of play". The game, between Dunmore and Strathmore, was played eleven-a-side, with a goalkeeper, two backs, two half-backs, and six forwards, and in September of that year, the SFA meeting, with a Dundee representative present, announced that there were now 91 clubs in the Association, an increase of 23 since the previous year. Rugby and Football were going their separate ways — and the operation was sometimes painful. In a match between Vale of Strathmore (Coupar Angus) and Dunkeld, which was theoretically played under Association rules, one of the Strathmore team had an arm dislocated, another bore "visible marks of rough treatment", and a third was unable to finish the game. The *Advertiser* commented that the rules "must have been disobeyed".

In the west, however, the game was flourishing. Twenty thousand had watched Vale of Leven defeat Glasgow Rangers in the 1877 Scottish Cup Final, and in 1878, Glasgow outfitters, R W Forsyth, began to advertise "football costumes" in the Dundee newspaper. "Jerseys, hose, belts, caps, cowls and knickerbockers" were all available by post from the Renfield Street shop which claimed to supply "over 300 clubs". This, more than anything else, confirmed that football was becoming big business throughout Central Scotland. By the end of the decade at least three more clubs had added their name to the growing list in Dundee. They were Our Boys (founded 1877), East End (also founded 1877) and Dundee Harp, who were formed in 1879.

2

THE LAST TWENTY years of the nineteenth century were traumatic for the British people. The Victorian era of expansion was drawing to a close and, curiously, an event in Dundee helped to bring this realisation home. On the night of Sunday 28 December 1879, the high girders, or central section, of the Tay Bridge — at that time the longest railway bridge in the world — collapsed in a high wind, taking with them an engine, six coaches and seventy-five passengers. The event, according to historian John Prebble, shook the British Empire to its very foundations, since it destroyed the Victorians' smug pride and their belief in their own creative infallibility. One intrepid *Advertiser* reporter managed to keep his head, however. In the detached manner for which certain East Coast newspapers were to become famous, he reported that a match played between Arbroath and Glasgow Wanderers on New Year's Day 1880 (i.e. four days after the disaster) "was advertised to commence at 2.30 pm, but owing to the Glasgow players having lost the connecting train at Dundee . . ." began late. "A strong gale," he continued imperviously, "blew from the commencement of the match which towards the end increased almost to a hurricane". What style!

The effect of this great trauma was a kind of preparation for the new world which change was about to bring and the 1880s and 1890s also witnessed first the adoption of football by the working classes as their national game and then its transition from casual amateur status to organised professionalism and the object of a kind of religious fervour.

14

The High Land, an early "multi" built c. 1870 to house Jute workers. The more traditional Jute worker's house, the one-storey tenement, is in the foreground.
(Courtesy: Dundee Public Library)

West Craigie Park. Now bordered by Morgan Place, Park Avenue, Baxter Park Terrace and "Tayside Works". This was the venue of the first professional football game played in Dundee – Dundee FC v Rangers, 1893. Harp also played there.
(Courtesy: D Coutts)

15

Leisure time had been hard won and if the Victorian promise of eternal prosperity through hard work and faith in the Lord was not to be fulfilled then, metaphorically speaking, the freedom train was approaching Wormit, and the wind was getting up. . . .

It was then that men in their frantic escapist search first discovered the spiritual qualities of football, for although to play at the highest level was the achievement of few it was the aspiration of many. Merely watching its matches brought a new kind of release, a new kind of solidarity and a new kind of sociability. Plus, of course, the fact that there might be a job of work at the end of the line, or indeed a business investment, did not go entirely unnoticed.

At the beginning of the 1880s, however, the game was still strictly amateur and the quaint names of some of the local clubs bore testament to the Corinthian spirit. There were "Perseverance", "Try Again" and a particular favourite was "Our Boys", with teams from Brechin, Blairgowrie, Arbroath, Dunfermline and Dundee all adopting that title. Originally it had been a nickname given to Glasgow Rangers during the seventies and was probably the origin of the expression "The Boys" as in "C'mon the Boys!" The first match between Our Boys (Dundee) and East End (Dundee) took place on Saturday 24 February 1880. It was an occasion which was eagerly anticipated and the teams met on a local farmer's land, Lawton Park. Tapes were used instead of crossbars at this time, and Our Boys won by two goals to nil. Their colours were red and black stripes with white shorts, but in 1882 they changed to the now more familiar dark blue jerseys and white shorts and acquired a "home" pitch at West Craigie Park, on farmland to the west of Baxter Park. (The Tayside works later expanded northwards to cover part of this ground and Morgan Place was built on another part in 1937.) East End, meanwhile, who played in blue and white stripes, made their home ground Clepington Park near the present site of Tannadice and the Harp (green jerseys, harp on breast, dark shorts) acquired their own Harp Athletic Grounds in East Dock Street, near the large gas tanks.

Both Harp and Hibernians (Dundee) had been established to cater for the immigrant Irish population of Dundee. In 1861, out of a population of approximately 100,000, between fourteen and fifteen thousand were Irish-born citizens attracted by the prospect of work in the rapidly expanding jute industry. This was roughly the same proportion as existed in Glasgow at the time but whereas in that city, or indeed Greenock, Edinburgh or Aberdeen there were more Irish males than females, in Dundee there were twice as many women as men.

Now according to William Walker, author of *Juteopolis*, Dundee appears to have attracted only the Catholic Irish, but the fact that there were more women than men, that Dundee was a Liberal "frontier town" where anti-Irish prejudice would be no more serious than, say, prejudice against Highlanders or country folk from Fife or Angus, and perhaps most significant, that membership of Orange Lodges was very small and politically unimportant, went a long way to explaining the relative absence of Irish sectarianism in the city. Also, socially, the two nations which existed in Dundee were not Scots and Irish, or Protestant and Catholic, but rich and poor, for while some inhabited mansions in the West End or Broughty Ferry, virtually all the others shared the tenements in conditions which were grim even by the standards of comparable industrial towns. The infantile death-rate in these tenements was ten times as high as in the suburbs, and the general physical, moral and mental degradation contributed to the need for some kind of diversion and improvement. In 1873, the Catholic community which by then owned a number of churches and schools, acquired a "Young Men's Hall" in Tay Street. This was designed for the purposes of recreation and education and was said to be the finest in Dundee. It was therefore but a short step to establish a football club with its own grounds.

The Forfarshire Football Association was formed in 1883 at the initiative of the leading Dundee clubs and consisted in its first season of eighteen teams — twelve from Dundee, two from Arbroath, one each from Montrose, Broughty Ferry and Lochee (the "dark village" which was slowly being converted by the jute-owning Cox family into an industrial suburb) and one from Coupar Angus, two of whose forwards went by the name of Gilzean. The first Forfarshire Cup was won by Arbroath who defeated Harp 2 1 in the final, and when another cup was presented to the Association by the Dundee Burns Club, local rivalry became greatly intensified.

Our Boys and East End were the clubs which made the early running with each turning out up to three teams per week, but the real success story was that of Harp whose hat-trick of Forfarshire Cup victories in the 1880s (1884-85, 1885-86, 1886-87) earned them the nickname "The Invincibles" in the Glasgow press. The standard of football,

17

however, was still lower than in the west, for although they reached the fourth round of the Scottish Cup in 1884-85, they lost 6-0 to Vale of Leven. On the east coast, though, they ranked second only to Edinburgh Hibs at this time (Dundee Hibs were erased from the SFA roll before season 1884-85) and whereas many schoolboys know that the record score in Scottish football is Abroath's 36-0 defeat of Bon Accord (Aberdeen) on the 12 September 1885, how many know that the second highest score was achieved by Harp in the same round of the Scottish Cup? That same day Harp beat Aberdeen Rovers 35-0, and according to the sporting press, it could have been more! At least Aberdonians can take some comfort from the fact that, one hundred years on, footballing standards in their home town have improved somewhat.

The year 1885 must go down as one of the most significant in the city of Dundee's footballing history. The week after their record breaking performance, Harp met Our Boys at East Dock Street in the second round of the Forfarshire Cup. The "bible" of Scottish sport, the Glasgow-based *Scottish Umpire* compared the crowd of 10,000 people to that at an international, and in losing 3-1 to their great rivals, Our Boys must have been bitterly disappointed. So much so, in fact, that some two months later deep-seated differences between the players and the committee came to the surface and resulted in a strike by Our Boys' players against their committee, with the players demanding the resignation of the "old and popular president" of the club, Mr J M Dron. The committee, however, held firm, and when two players — Buttars and Porter — changed their minds, a new team was quickly assembled around them.

But the damage was done, and the result was that the other players severed their connection with the club and started a new combination under the name of the "Wanderers". Their nickname was "The Forkies" possibly because they had "forked off" from Our Boys. The voice of the sporting establishment, the *Scottish Umpire* commented that "the plucky management of 'the Boys' committee will remain as a standing memorial of what a few able and right-minded men can do". Revolution, it would seem was not popular with the editor, who went on to remark that even the very name chosen by the new club was a "suggestive soubriquet". Whatever might be in a name, however, this rift was to prove bitter, irreconcilable, and arguably the historical basis of Dundee's development as a divided footballing city.

Dundee c. 1890. The Junction of the High Street and Overgate. The Telegraph Office was in Thorter Row which ran from Melville House (left) to Overgate (right). Football fans would gather at their "own" place to await results

First of all, the struggle for pre-eminence in the town became a four-cornered one between Our Boys, East End, Wanderers and Harp, but this was increasingly overshadowed by a new factor, for as clubs broadened their appeal, more and more people began to identify with one or other particular team. As the pressure to win increased, so did the competition for the best local players, and this in turn led to clubs paying the best players to come and play for them. Thus the small local clubs were forced along a road to *professionalism* which was legalised first in England in 1885.

Professionalism existed in other sports at the time, notably boxing and cycling, but it had a bad reputation owing to the gambling it attracted. Professional cricket, however, had managed to maintain its dignity and this became the model for English clubs faced with the issue. Soon the top English clubs were visiting Scotland for holiday fixtures at New Year or Easter and this in turn led to the first wholesale plundering of Scottish football by their wealthy neighbours.

The SFA initially stood firmly against what it called the "unmitigated evil of professionalism" and "even Parnell," said the *Scottish Umpire*, "could not have uttered more acrid denunciations against the land of the rose". The Scottish football establishment more or less got its own way until season 1890-91 when a case of professionalism was proved against St Bernards of Edinburgh and

19

they were suspended for six weeks. It was the opinion of the SFA that the club then simply made a few cosmetic changes and changed their name to Edinburgh Saints, so when Renton (Champions of the World, 1888) applied to play the Saints, permission was refused. Renton, however, went ahead, and both clubs were expelled, which meant that they were effectively banned from the new Scottish League too. Renton sued the SFA and achieved an out-of-court victory which resulted in an amnesty for professionals in Scotland. Of course, the whole thing was a sham in that players throughout the country were being paid, but given that, the Dundee clubs had suffered very badly as a result of English professionalism, and none worse than Harp, whose match secretary, a Mr James Diamond, believed that if they had all their English players reinstated, they would be one of the best clubs in Scotland. Replying to a *Scottish Sport* (*Scottish Umpire* became *Scottish Sport* in 1888) editorial on Dundee which railed against disgraceful grounds, petty personal dignities, club jealousies and, significantly, the fact that there were too many senior clubs in the town (the editor suggested two), Diamond replied that it was not the number of clubs but the activities of the "English agent" which prevented Dundee clubs from taking their rightful place at the top table of Scottish football. Indeed he suggested then that an amnesty would be the best course.

Mr Diamond and his club had had a difficult few years. In January 1887, when still the best team in Forfarshire, Harp were involved in an incident which served to blacken their reputation. Having been drawn away to a leading west coast club, Dumbarton, in the third round of the Scottish Cup, Harp elected to scratch but, expecting a good gate, offered Dumbarton a £20 guarantee to play the match as a friendly in Dundee. Dumbarton agreed and, anticipating the usual 12.45 kick-off, were surprised to learn just after noon, as they sat in their hotel, that the kick-off time was in fact 12.15. The players rushed to the ground but when they arrived they discovered that Harp had told the (small) crowd that Dumbarton had failed to turn up and had given them their money back. To make matters worse the game had been advertised as the Scottish Cup tie and when the *Umpire* raised the point, Diamond blamed the misunderstanding on his superiors who, he claimed, would not allow him to take the words "Scottish Cup 3rd round" off the bills. In any event, the Harp executive, including Diamond, were dismissed. The *Umpire* mercilessly pursued the club and its "inner circle" through its columns for the next few years by continually alluding to the incident.

Harp now went into a period of decline and in 1890 another stick was found with which to beat it. Glasgow Celtic were founded in 1887-88 and like Harp were initially a secrarian club inasmuch as all their players and officials were Roman Catholics, mostly of Irish origin. Celtic were founded as a charity for the relief of the poor in Glasgow's east end but in the 1890s commercial pressures dictated that they become first a limited liability company and then that they sign the best players irrespective of their religion or background. In 1895, a motion was put forward that the number of Protestants in the team should be limited to three, but this was defeated by a counter-motion that the committee should have the right to sign as many Protestants as they wished. From that day forth, Celtic Football Club has been a non-sectarian organisation.

In the late 1880s, the issue of sectarianism in sport did not appear to concern the establishment, or at least the editor of the *Umpire*. "We learn," he wrote in November 1887, "that the efforts which have lately been made to organise a first class Catholic Club have been consummated. We wish the Celts all success". This attitude, however, was to change and the change coincided with Celtic's rapid rise to prominence. By November 1890, when they visited Our Boys (Dundee), Celtic were one of Scotland's leading clubs, and the occasion was described as the "most important event . . . in the history of Northern football". A crowd of 4,000 saw Celtic defeat the "Blues" 3-1 at West Craigie where for the first time a special room had been set aside for the press. Not least impressed by this new (sectarian) club were the powers behind Harp.

Discouraged by the loss of nine players to England that year, the Harp executive had taken a decision to play a "mixed" eleven of Scots and Irish in an attempt to restore the club's fortunes, and a new secretary, Charles Mulholland, had been appointed in September 1890 for the forthcoming season. Following the great impression which Celtic made, however, this policy was thrown overboard, the Scots players were abandoned and at a meeting of members and supporters on 26 November 1890, an effort was made to reorganise the club.[1] Senior officials, the Rev Monseignor Clapperton, Rev Fathers Holder, Harris and Van de Rydt decided "that the club should in future be run on the same principle as the Celtic" and a telegram was received from

Celtic wishing them every success under their new management. *Scottish Sport* commented that "with such a large Irish constituency as that to be found in Dundee, we can imagine no better field for a first class Irish team and with the influence of the Roman Catholic clergy at its head, its sectarian success can be almost assured". Now whether this prospect caused him a sleepless night is uncertain, but the editor followed this three days later with a rather different editorial. He began by outlining the history of the club and its recent (chequered) past, but said that he believed the right men had now come forward. The new Honorary Presidents were Fathers Holder and Harris, and Diamond had been reinstated as the match secretary. It was his conclusion, however, which was of particular interest:

> While we welcome the reconstruction of the Harp we are sorry that it has been deemed advisable to run the management under the patronage of the church. We do not believe in clubs formed on sectarian lines; it does the cause of religion more harm than good and it brings the charity and humanity of sport into a narrow channel for the outflow of tolerance and the coarse feelings of our everyday life. The Harp, by following the lines of Celtic are introducing into Dundee and the north of Scotland, a phase of football which we happen to know does not have the sanction or support of some of the finest and most Catholic minds of the Romish church.

On 6 December 1890 Harp turned out an entirely "Irish" team for the first time in almost a year. In front of a poor crowd, they defeated Strathmore 1-0.

NOTES

1 — Another factor which would have influenced the churchmen in their decision to become involved in the running of the Harp Club was the storm which was then raging over Parnell's leadership of Sinn Fein.

Following great success, Parnell was cited in a divorce case and the Catholic Church came down heavily in favour of his resignation. Perhaps they felt it was their duty to try and ensure that their moral values were upheld by the young Catholic community in the town. With a few notable exceptions, Presbyterian and Episcopalean ministers paid little attention to football and some openly opposed it.

3

THE ISSUE OF sectarianism has never dominated football in Dundee and so it was in the Juteopolis at this time. East End (the "Wise Men") reached the sixth round of the Scottish Cup in season 1889-90 and won the Burns Cup. And Our Boys went with them all the way, taking the Forfarshire goblet in 1889-90 and 1890-91. For the first time (though not the last) there were rumblings of favouritism by the SFA for west coast clubs when it came to handing out international "caps" and no case was more spectacular than that of William Dickson (Strathmore) who was the first footballer from a Dundee club to play for Scotland. Dickson was in fact a Fifer from Crail who became a top-class centre-forward with Strathmore and, following some pressure by the *Umpire*, was picked to play against Ireland in 1888. In a 10-2 victory he scored no less than four goals but (perhaps unremarkably) was never selected again. In a distinguished career he then moved to Sunderland, Aston Villa (he was an FA Cup Finalist in 1892) and finally Stoke with whom he was a player, coach, and ultimately a director. Dickson was the first real football personality in Dundee and when he returned during close seasons, his movements were eagerly followed by the press who reported him once as having been spotted "fishing for flooks" at Invergowrie. One can't see Charlie Nicholas having the same interest in flat fish, but if he did it would doubtless be put before the public and with the same justification in the 1980s as the 1890s.

Meanwhile Wanderers were managing to establish themselves alongside the "bigger" clubs locally. Having made their home Morgan Park (off Mains Loan and connected to Morgan Academy, or Hospital as it was in 1886 a boarding school for fatherless boys) they opened a grandstand there in season 1887-88 and reached the quarter-finals of the Scottish Cup. They also won the Burns Cup in 1886-87 and 1887-88 and at least three of their players, Henry, Duncan and Moodie, joined the exodus south. In December 1890, however, they faced a challenge of a different nature. Alex Batchelor, a farmer of West Craigie estate which housed Morgan Park, sued the club for £28.00 as rent in arrears. A decree in absence was pronounced with the proviso that if security was obtained within a fortnight, the club would have three months in which to pay their debt. It would seem the matter could not be satisfactorily resolved, however, for Wanderers lost the tenancy of Morgan Park and moved to Clepington Park which had been vacated in turn by East End when they moved to Pitkerro Park, near the present home of Stobswell Juniors. In the early months of the following year, 1891, as if to make a fresh start, the club changed its name to Johnstone Wanderers[1] and at a meeting of the Dundee Burns Charity Association on 3 March, the "new" club was represented by a Mr J Gamble.

By this time the highly successful new Scottish League was reaching its first climax (Dumbarton and Rangers would share the first Championship) and the formation of a Northern League was proposed since the leading Scottish clubs were now only visiting the north at New Year, and the game was deteriorating locally — although another Forfarshire player, the Dundee-born Alex Keillor (Montrose) was about to receive his first cap, against Wales. The first general meeting of the Northern League was held in Mathers Temperance Hotel (now the Tay Hotel) on Saturday 4 April 1891. A Mr Duncan (Our Boys) seconded by Mr Spalding of East End suggested a league of eight clubs. Mr Diamond of Harp, however, seconded by Mr Gamble of Johnstone Wanderers, suggested ten as both these clubs feared they might be excluded if only eight were elected. Their fears were well-founded, for only three Dundee clubs were to gain admission and in the ballot Harp defeated Johnstone Wanderers by 14 votes to 6. The clubs elected were Montrose, Arbroath, Forfar Athletic, Our Boys, East End, Harp, St Johnstone and Aberdeen, and the exclusion of Johnstone Wanderers rather surprised the editor of *Scottish Sport*. Although the voting suggested that blame for this could not entirely be laid at Our Boys door, he concluded that the "old hatred" seemed likely to be rekindled and that Johnstone Wanderers would vow vengeance "on the heads of those who were

Dundee Harp c. 1885 with Forfarshire Cup and Dundee Burns Cup.
Back Row: Phin, Murray, Lees, John Hogan (Chairman), McTaggart,
Murphy, Rock.
Front Row: McGirl, M D'Arcy Sen (Black Mick), M D'Arcy Jun (Big Mick),
Gilmartin, Connolly.
Peter Rock was a founder and Star Player.
"(In 1879) there was an excursion going to Springfield and to help the day's
diversion the boys of St Joseph's school arranged a football match with the
lads of St Andrew's Church. The St Joseph's lot took the name of the 'Hibs'
and so to be upsides with them we called ourselves 'The Harp'. Well, we gave
them a beating and they took it that sore that on the next Saturday when we
went down to the Magdalen Green to have another tussle, they would not let
us play with them. 'Awa' and buy a ball for yerself', they shouted and we took
their advice and went off and constituted The Harp as a Club."
Dundee Harp pre-dated Glasgow Celtic by eight or nine years, and Rock it
was who raised the green flag at Tannadice on the foundation of Dundee Hibs
in 1909. Curiously, St Joseph's school also retained their connection with one
share in the Dundee Hibs and Dundee United Companies.

(Courtesy: Lochee Harp Junior Football Club)

instrumental in procuring their exclusion". They did not allow this vow to interfere with their progress, however, and in an attempt to keep up with East End who now leased a new recreation ground at Carolina Port from the Harbour Trustees, they embarked on an ambitious scheme to improve Clepington Park.

The new ground was to be opened on 2 May 1891, with a game against Broughty Ferry, but the "fireside sailors" failed to turn up and Clepington Park retained its virgin charms until the following week, when Raith Rovers did the honours. "Like Morgan Park," said *Scottish Sport*, "the new enclosure has a slope but not nearly so pronounced." There was no grandstand, but "plenty of room for one" and "everything considered", the Wanderers "were to be congratulated on having secured such comfortable quarters after encountering so many difficulties". The park was opened by Bailie Stevenson and by the kind of coincidence that makes life interesting, that same week a young Dundee junior team, Strathmore Athletic, announced that they had decided to give themselves the somewhat pretentious title of Dundee United. The new stadium at Clepington Park, of course, was to become the home of the "real" Dundee United, Tannadice Park.

Season 1891-92, the second of the Scottish League and the first of the Northern League, was also the first season of the professional amnesty. It made little difference to the flow of players south, but some technical improvements were being made in the way the game was played, in the field of play, and in the rules of the game. Over the next few years, football would begin to look more like the thing we know today, with the introduction of crossbars and goal-nets, the number of opponents in the offside rule being established as three, the penalty kick being introduced, and "hacking" outlawed. Players still had to "claim" for a foul or goal, however, which would stand if one of the "umpires" (linesmen) raised his stick and the referee blew his whistle. There was still no penalty box, merely a twelve-yard line.

East End moved into the Carolina Port ground and Strathmore into Logie Park in Scott Street. Our Boys were offered exemption from the Scottish Cup but chose to play (against Harp) and lost 2-0. In a reported incident which reflects the depth of feeling between the clubs, and also the social habits of the supporters in an age long before television, the Wanderers' players on returning to Dundee from their game in Perth, "went to a corner in High Street" which was "sacred to

Our Boys and their supporters" and shouted, "Three cheers for the Harp!" (Supporters apparently would wait in High Street near the telegraph office in Thorter Row for results of their team's match, with each set having their own place.) The same issue of *Scottish Sport* also welcomed the Harp revival and in yet another about-face wrote, "As an improving factor, there is nothing in Dundee to equal a successful Irish organisation." In spite of these inconsistencies, however, it was not above reproaching others for unprofessional conduct. D C Thomson's *Courier* came under fire in the 1880s for plagiarising the *Umpire's* Dundee notes, and the *Evening Telegraph* was later criticised for abandoning its "Sporting Pink" over the summer months. "Dundee," said the *Umpire*, "deserved better".

Some other social comments from this publication also give an insight into contemporary life. "Football Special" trains, for example,

Dundee FC 1895
Standing: Marshall (Trainer), Darroch, Barrett, Fleming.
Middle Row: Dundas, Longair, Keillor.
Front Row: Thomson, McInroy, Maxwell, Sawers, Gilligan.
(Courtesy: *Scottish Sport*, Mitchell Library DC Thomson)

were begun in the 1880s and 1890s, although sometimes players themselves could not get to matches if they had to work on a Saturday. As if to remind the historian that this really was a different time, and the end of an era, *Scottish Sport* in November 1891 advertised the forthcoming appearance of none other than Buffalo Bill, whose Wild West Show played at the East End Exhibition Hall in the city's Duke Street.

Football was an even bigger attraction, however, and even the prospect of increased admission charges from 3d to 4d or 6d did not have any deterrent effect. At the time a "big offer" to a Dundee player (Dundas, Our Boys) from a top English club (Sheffield Wednesday) was £3.10s. a week. Celtic won the 1891-92 Scottish Cup, Dumbarton the League, and the first Northern League Championship was shared by Our Boys and East End. It was also decided to increase the Northern League membership from eight to ten clubs and Johnstone Wanderers and Victoria United (Aberdeen) were elected for season 1892-93. In 1892 Lochee United (who were said to have a close relationship with Harp) opened their new ground near South Road, and could field a team entirely of Lochee men. They were looked upon as a senior team at this time and junior clubs like East Craigie and Violet were the province of younger players.

Leading the field in terms of amenities were East End, whose new ground at Carolina Port was comparable to anything in the west and able to accomodate 1,500 people in the stand, 1,000 at the rail, and up to 10,000 on the bank. The pitch itself was also splendid with separate running and cycle tracks. And they had a team to match. Following a 5-1 victory against Our Boys their goalkeeper, Ure, was "courted" by the West Craigie club, where it was said he would meet "fellows like himself — travellers, clerks etc. — which would be far better than mixing with such a common rough lot as the Carolina Port crowd". Our Boys obviously considered themselves a better "class" of team, but Ure stayed put, and there was no shortage of money to keep him there, for at a home friendly match against Sunderland the "gate" was a staggering £104.00, from a 3d admission charge.

The issue of professionalism in Scotland now really began to gear up and Johnstone Wanderers, not to be left behind, built a grandstand at Clepington Park. Gates were said to be decreasing at the turn of the year however due to dull trade, bad weather, and the number of friendlies the local teams played against each other, and when Our

Boys' stand at West Craigie Park burned down, football in the town hit something of a low ebb. By the Spring, though, all this was changing.

On 24 March 1893, *Scottish Sport* contained a report:

> Communications have been passing between two leading Dundee clubs over amalgamation and asking admittance to the Scottish League. At present the matter is being kept as secret as possible but from small indications observed, there is little chance of it being successfully carried out.

The two clubs were Our Boys and East End and the suggestion prompted a great deal of talk locally. The general opinion was that any other two clubs might unite and work in harmony, but that Our Boys and East End never could. Nothing, however, is certain in football and events now overtook opinion in Dundee.

At a revolutionary meeting of the SFA on 2 May 1893, the legalisation of professionalism was proposed by the dynamic Mr J McLaughlin of Celtic. Professionalism existed, he said, and everyone knew it, and in a revealing rejoinder he added that as things stood, players were masters of clubs. With the advent of professionalism, he argued, "Clubs would now be masters of players and standards would rise . . . whether or not they approved of professionalism they should control it". The motion was seconded by J Gamble of Johnstone Wanderers and passed. "Exit bogus amateurism," said *Scottish Sport* in another fantastic U-turn, "enter honest professionalism".

The majority of the Forfarshire clubs were against legalisation as they thought the struggling clubs would be ruined but in Dundee incredulity concerning the amalgamation was giving way to pragmatism and supporters of both clubs now focused their attention on what most were beginning to see as a positive, indeed lifesaving move. There were dissenters, of course, but the officials of the two clubs continued to hold discussions. East End at that time were favourites to win the Northern League and had to beat Harp in the final game of the season to take the flag (20 May 1893). They lost 4-2, however, and the all-conquering, all-local Arbroath team of that year beat them into second place with Harp fifth, Johnstone Wanderers seventh, and Our Boys eighth out of ten.

That evening, an application was drafted for presentation at the Scottish League AGM on Monday 12 June:

We, the undersigned as representing the Our Boys and East End clubs of Dundee, hereby make application for admittance as an amalgamated club to be named the Dundee Football Club to membership of the Scottish Football League.

We beg to submit that this application on behalf of the two leading clubs of this district has the entire sympathy of the general public and that committees and players of both clubs are prepared to give the new club their support.

Should this application receive your favourable consideration, we would point out to you the advantages financially of the scheme. Matches between local clubs at threepence for admission have drawn over £100.00 at the gates and we feel sure that with the admission raised to sixpence, and with interest attaching to a national competition such as the Scottish League, that this sum could be easily doubled.

One visit per annum from each of the league clubs would revive interest in the game here and would ensure large attendances.

Dundee, being the third largest centre of population in Scotland, viz 200,000 will, we think, commend itself favourably to you as a centre for a Scottish League Club.

Dundee is now within easy reach of Edinburgh and Glasgow having connections with both the Caledonian and North British Railways. There is at the disposal of the new club a ground with a playing pitch of 120 yards long by 75 yards broad, quite level and well turfed. Accommodation is provided for 20,000 spectators.

We are certain that we can sustain the interest in the competition throughout the entire season, as we have a large field in the North of Scotland from which to engage players to compose our team.

SIGNED Wm Black.
Thomas Shaw *East End FC*
Andw Williamson
John Cameron *Our Boys*

(and A Buttar also signed the original document).

Amalgamation hinged on admission to the Scottish League, and *Scottish Sport*[2] commented that the application should be supported. When the news arrived in Dundee on the Monday night that the new club was in at the head of the League poll, any reservations which the respective supporters had were magically dissolved, and some even danced in the High Street! The *Dundee Advertiser* marked the occasion with the following report:

On Monday June 12 1893 the Annual General Meeting of the Scottish Football League was held in Glasgow. The balance sheet showed a large surplus, and the office-bearers were all re-elected. Thereafter, the representatives of Renton, Abercorn and Clyde — the clubs which had fewest points — retired, and applications for admission were made by St Bernards, Hibernian (Edinburgh) and the newly-formed Dundee. The final division resulted in an equal number of votes being given for Renton and Dundee, while the last vacancy went to St Bernards. The Scottish League first division now comprised Celtic, Rangers, Third Lanark, St Mirren, Dumbarton, Renton, Hearts, St Bernards, Leith Ath and Dundee. Mr William Black represented the newly-admitted club from the north.

The editor then opined:

> The new step will doubtless give a great impetus to the sport in Dundee. The new Club has been formed by the amalgamation of Our Boys and East End, the object being to raise a team which, while thoroughly representative, will be capable of upholding the city's honour in the football field and which will be able to take a front place in the national competition.

Suitably Victorian sentiments, and the writer also remarked that the other nine clubs would in future have to come to Dundee in "full strength" and not as apparently had often been the case with friendly fixtures in Dundee, with a weak team. He concluded that Dundonians "will next season have opportunities of witnessing all the most famous Scottish exponents of the game".

Dundee had arrived as a footballing city.

NOTES

1 — A club called Johnstone Athletic had played at Fairmuir. The name may have related to a local estate or farm.

2 — *Scottish Sport* carried the following report in their edition of 23 June 1893: "The Dundee FC is now an accomplished fact. A general meeting of the East End was held on Monday night when it was resolved to wind up their affairs and join with Our Boys to form the new body. Six-members were chosen to represent them, and these gentlemen and their representatives met representatives of Our Boys on Tuesday evening (20 June) in Mathers Hotel, and the office-bearers in the new club were elected. The principle of election carried out was to choose members from the two

clubs alternatively to fill the various offices. The following is the list:

President: James Petrie (East End)
Vice President: A Buttar (Our Boys)
Business Secretary: W Black
Match Secretary: A Williamson
Jt. Treasurers: J MacLean & J M Forbes
Sel. of 'A' team: D MacVicar
Commitee: T McKee, A Spalding, W Saunders, J MacIntosh, W K Murray.

4

Welcome! thrice welcome! to the year 1893,
For it is the year that I intend to leave Dundee.
Owing to the treatment I receive
Which does my heart sadly grieve.
Every morning when I got out
The ignorant rabble they do shout
'There goes mad McGonagall'
In derisive shouts as loud as they can bawl
And lifts stones and snowballs, throws them at me;
And such actions are shameful to be heard in the
City of Dundee.

—New Year's Resolution to leave Dundee

Wm McGonagall *b*. Edinburgh 1825 *d*. Edinburgh 1903

SEASON 1893-94 was the first played in Scotland under profession-alism and all in all it was deemed a great success. For the next few years, however, patrons in Dundee might have been excused for thinking they were at the Gussie Park Carnival rather than their favourite football ground, such was the merry-go-round of soccer in the city. Harp, for example, while accepting professionalism, felt they simply could not afford to pay players unless the home club received all the gate money and put forward a motion to that effect at a special meeting of the Northern League. Further, they required an increase in admission charges to 4d for adults and 2d for juveniles, but it was generally recognised that only the second proposal would receive the sanction of the committee and so the feeling was that Harp's letter was effectively one of resignation. Indeed Mr Diamond had gone so far as to state that they "were not anxious to enter the League" that season and although they recruited some new men from the West, they eventually decided to resign and were replaced by Strathmore.

Strathmore was thought to be the oldest surviving football club in the town and they proceeded to cause a minor sensation by securing the lease for Carolina Port, which had been expected to go to the new amalgamation. Dundee FC, therefore, began its life in the rather less auspicious surroundings of West Craigie Park. But this in no way detracted from the sense of occasion at the opening match against Glasgow Rangers on Saturday the "glorious" twelfth of August 1893. There was great excitement in the town and by two o'clock the crowd was streaming along Arbroath Road. Ultimately, between four and five thousand people assembled and they apparently got good value for their 6d admission fee, witnessing a 3-3 draw. Dundee lined up: McKie, Ferrier and Brown; Craig, Longair and Petrie; Thomson, Craik, Dundas, Gilligan and Keillor (the international "cap" who had joined from Montrose). The *Advertiser* commented, "Thus has Dundee been successfully launched on its League career".[1]

The West Craigie Park was not a long-term proposition, however, and following a number of defeats the Dundee committee decided to stage a business "coup" by buying a controlling interest in the Athletic Grounds Company which was in financial difficulty. This put Strathmore in an invidious position and early in 1894 they decided to amalgamate with Johnstone Wanderers at Clepington Park in an attempt to provide the city with a second top-class club. The name they chose for the new combination was Dundonians FC but Dundee FC objected, claiming (understandably) that they were already being referred to in the national press as "the Dundonians". Otherwise, however, Dundee FC were said to welcome the new amalgamation and when their objection was upheld by the SFA, the Clepington Park club decided to opt for the "Wanderers" as their name. Their colours were red and white shirts and blue shorts.

Harp, meanwhile, who themselves had long harboured ambitions of becoming a top club, were slipping farther into difficulty through mismanagement and a failure to meet their financial obligations to other clubs, and on 3 April 1894, they were suspended by the SFA for

The Opening of Dens Park 19 August 1899; Dundee FC v St Bernards.
Dundee FC (white jerseys): T Stewart; Watson and White; Baird, Longair
and Keillor; T Low, Steven, Robertson, McDiarmid, A Stewart.
The ground was opened by Lord Provost McGrady and McDiarmid scored for
Dundee in a 1-1 draw. The official party and players are depicted in front of
the South (Dens Road) Stand, which was transferred from Carolina Port.

non-payment of guarantees. There was immediately a rumour that a new Irish club might appear in the hands of men of "higher social standing" and in September 1894 such a club did appear — to be known as the Dundee Hibs. In order to circumvent the stigma which attached in official circles to the name Harp, a statement was issued that there were none of the executive of the defunct club on the committee of the new organisation, and with the following officials, the club set up home at West Craigie: President: John Fagan; Vice President: J Flood; Financial Secretary: P Doyle; Treasurer: J MacLaren; Match Secretary: Frank Carroll.

Wanderers (represented by President: D Reid; Vice President: J Duncan; Joint Treasurers: J Alexander and J McCulloch; Financial Secretary: D MacEwan; and Match Secretary: J MacLeod) were also elected to the new Scottish Second Division in 1894, but they ran into trouble almost immediately by losing the tenancy of Clepington Park and although they found a new home at East Dock Street (Harp's old ground), their bad luck did not abate, and when they finished second bottom of the Second Division, they failed to be re-elected. Dundee FC, however, continued to put up a good performance in the First Division, and finished eighth of ten in each of their first two seasons. Relations had also improved between the two clubs to such an extent that Dundee actually loaned their old rivals money at one stage — a gesture thought noteworthy by the Glasgow press — and in signing the ex-Harp goalkeeper, Francis Barrett, the club showed an immediate willingness to go for the best players, whatever their religion. Besides, it was good business to have a popular "Irishman" in the side and Barrett went on to become one of Dundee FC's first international "caps" along with Longair and Keillor, for Scotland against Ireland in 1894.

The 1894-95 season also saw Dundee's first successful Scottish Cup run for, having defeated the mighty Celtic in an earlier round and for record gate money, the Dark Blues went on to contest an epic, three-match semi-final with Renton before finally going down 3-0.[2] The returns, and not for the last time, showed the club the financial value of a good run in the Scottish Cup but even this much-needed finance and success was not enough to enable them to hold on to their star centre-forward Maxwell who was enticed by a local scout to join Dickson at Stoke, and who went on to become the first Dundonian to play for Scotland against England, in 1898.

So the "carnival" continued. Wanderers returned to Clepington Park; Dundee Hibs became Harp again in 1895, had the name ratified by the SFA at the second attempt and moved back to Dock Street; and Dundee FC witnessed serious hooliganism for the first time. Following a game with Hearts at Tynecastle on 2 November 1895, a crowd of about one thousand Hearts supporters congregated outside the pavilion to remonstrate with a young Dundee forward called Vail, whose robust challenges had not met with their approval. Police were called and had to draw batons while Vail made his exit through the back door. It was said to be the first incident of its type in Edinburgh and the Hearts officials regretted it "exceedingly".

The fact that clubs could pay the price of admission to the "show", therefore, did not guarantee a joy ride, and Dundee FC were next to experience the effects of the roundabouts and swings of professionalism.

Although they were having their best season so far, there were indications of a cash crisis at Carolina Port shortly after New Year 1896, and one or two guarantees were said to be outstanding. The problem, said the *Sport*, was that although Dundee had done well in the League (they were to finish fifth in the First Division that season) they were out of the Scottish Cup, and with no prospects of lucrative friendlies against local rivals because of the inferiority of the opposition, the club had only its traditional holiday fixtures against English opposition to look forward to, and this could not pay the wages. The Glasgow paper, therefore, again called for a strong new club in the town and again it demonstrated its ambivalence on the issue of sectarianism. "If the new body has sectarian flavour," declared the editor, "so much the better, as the Irish population in Dundee is a very large one." This institutionalised ambivalence has continued to afflict the Scottish game. On the one hand sectarianism in sport is condemned while on the other, if it is seen to do no harm to a club's commercial prospects, it is overlooked, or even justified. At least it can be said that the Dundee clubs made some kind of attempt to resolve this dilemma (although some people would have liked Dundee FC in

Dens Park action c. 1905. The picture shows the old North Stand with Provost Road behind (left) and Clepington Road.

(Courtesy: Dundee Public Library)

particular to go farther) and in fairness, the *Sport* recognised even then whatever a club's policies, it still has to produce a first-class team to enjoy success.

At a meeting of the committee on 27 January 1896, Dundee FC told their players that their wages were to be reduced. The club was not in immediate danger but future payments were such that if expenses were not cut forthwith then trouble would be inevitable. There was talk of a players' revolt, but in the end only one player, the captain Hendry, changed clubs as a result of the edict. The rent for Carolina Port was also causing problems, and Dundee were said to have their eye on a new field in the north end of the town — but not before the "Burning Mountain" (a shale bing near the Carolina Port ground which continued to smoulder) had its moment of glory when it formed the backdrop for the Scotland-Wales international played at Carolina Port in March 1896. The pitch was said to be in poor condition for the game, but the large crowd were well-disciplined, and the *Sport* once again called for a "second" team in Dundee, this time an amalgamation of Wanderers and Harp.

It was the city's "first" team, however, which was causing immediate concern, and matters came to a head on 23 April when a revolutionary grouping emerged at the Dundee AGM to launch an assault on the embattled committee. President Brown and Vice President Kidd, as non-party members, managed to hold on to their positions, but only two members of the old committee survived with them and the names of Williamson, Black and Petrie were replaced by Ireland, Andrews and Smellie. The first reaction of the old guard was to throw their lot behind the Wanderers and an application for membership of the Second Division went before the SFA on behalf of a new club, Dundee County. It was unsuccessful, but more would be heard from its sponsors; and Harp too were again in the throes of reorganisation with the familiar name of Diamond once more at the helm.

The new Dundee FC committee went about its business with great determination. Gilligan and Thomson went to Bolton, Longair and Burgess to Sunderland, and their replacments also came from across the border, most notably Kelso, a full-back from Everton who was later capped and his team-mate Jack Hillman, a goalkeeper, and the first Englishman to move to a Scottish League club. The new season (1896-97) was viewed with great optimism and, captained by Kelso and inspired by Hillman, the new team once again made a good start. So much so, in fact, that the club decided to follow the example of others and become a limited liability company, thereby raising some much-needed capital for present debt and future investment. The *Sport* suggested a subscribed capital of £1,000 in £1 shares, with a £5 directoral qualification so that the "working-class element" would *not* be eliminated from the management (again a change of tune), but when the first Dundee Athletic and Football Club *Limited* actually went on the market in March 1897, 2,000 £1 shares went on offer. Unfortunately the response from the public was poor with only 500 shares being taken up. Thus only temporary respite was achieved by "the Carolinas". Harp, too, had their problems. For one away game in Arbroath they only managed to raise three players and the prodigal Mr Diamond's efforts to have them registered by the SFA for various tournaments were invariably unsuccessful. But at least their expenses were minimal. Although fifth again in 1896-97, Dundee slipped to seventh place in 1897-98 and when they issued their balance sheet in March 1898 the extent of the difficulty was there for all to see. From an income of £3,265.2s.6d. wages of £1,912.12s.8d. had been paid, and by the time other expenses such as guarantees were met, the club showed a net loss of £222.9s.2d., even allowing for the new subscription of capital. In order to stave off the collapse which the close season would precipitate therefore, money had to be found, and indeed some local benefactors from the wine trade did come to the rescue. It was only temporary, however.

One again players were transferred wholesale and the club embarked upon season 1898-99 with a team which consisted largely of part-time local players. Even the great Hillman fell from grace. The big goalkeeper had been Dundee's most popular player since his arrival and stories about him were legion. Apparently his first landlady was a Gaelic speaker whom he couldn't understand, and when she laid a plate of porridge before him, he tackled it with a knife and fork! By the beginning of season 1898-99, however he was convinced he was being retained as a piece of financial speculation, and although he offered the club £100 for his own transfer (a large sum of money for an individual to raise in those days), they refused to budge. Hillman then took matters into his own hands and began to "play for his papers". First he pushed an indirect free-kick into his own net at Kilmarnock thus giving away a decisive goal. This, though, soon paled into insignificance when, in a derby match against the revived Wanderers, he first disputed a penalty decision and then leaned against a post as the kick was taken! Real "tough-of-the-track" stuff, and club suspension followed. Hillman finally took his case to the SFA meeting (from which he was eventually ejected) and later he returned to Lancashire when Burnley paid £200 for his transfer. A number of fans regretted the manner of his passing, writing to newspapers in his defence. He was subsequently capped by England.

Dundee's performances on the field, meanwhile, were deteriorating rapidly. After fourteen games they were bottom of the First Division with three points, and at 11 am on Friday 9 December 1898 they notified Celtic that their game the following day would have to be abandoned. The club, they said, was totally and irretrievably wrecked and although the *Sport* complained that they should have brought their shareholders together to give others a chance to save the club, it recognised that the long record of frustrated ambition could not go on and printed a short epitaph: "Thus ends an ill-starred venture." Ironically, the epitaph would have been more suited to *Scottish Sport* itself, for while Dundee FC revived and looked forward to a long life, the *Sport* was to go to the wall some sixteen months later.

The following poem also appeared:

BURIAL OF DUNDEE
by 'No XI'.

1 Who killed Dundee?
I, said the Celt
My power he felt
I killed Dundee.

2 Who saw him die?
I, said the Ranger
In his hour of danger
I saw him die.

3 Who'll be the parson?
I, said the Heart
It's a big-line part
I'll be the parson.

4 Who caught his blood?
I, said the Clyde
By the riverside
I caught his blood.

5 Who'll mollify the Co?
I, said the Hib
With words so glib
I'll mollify the Co.,

40

It was initially an intervention by the Scottish League which saved Dundee Football Club. At an emergency meeting on Wednesday 14 December, the league offered to guarantee the club their expenses, including wages, in the four remaining league games but this was refused, the directors being "sick of the whole affair" and having "definitely decided to go into liquidation". Also present at the same meeting, however, were two representatives of the earlier management, Mr Cameron and Mr Anderson. They were prepared to guarantee the continuance of the club under an enthusiastic and popular committee, given the League's offer. On 17 December 1898 Dundee Football and Athletic Club went into liquidation, but the idea of the new proprietors, said the *Sport*, was "at once to strike terms with the liquidators, and so make the club *not a new body, but merely a reorganised continuation,* thus obviating the necessity of transfer of players and allowing business to be continued". Also the word "limited" was to be dropped from the name and the outgoing directors apparently went to unexpected lengths to ensure a smooth transference of business. When the new committee was elected (on 20 December) it contained a number of familiar names including those of Williamson, Cameron, Petrie and Shaw. So Dundee's wheel of fortune had come full circle. With the opening of Dens Park in 1899 (300 yards up the road from Clepington Park), and the re-establishment of the club as a limited company in 1900,[4] Dundee FC was ready to take its place at the centre stage of Scottish football. Some years later it would be joined on that stage by another great club.

NOTES
1 — Sandy Gilligan was the scorer of Dundee FC's first goal, and the players received only 10/- per week initially.

2 — Dundee FC suffered the heaviest defeat in their history at Parkhead in 1895, with Longair concussed and off the field they went down 11-0.

3 — The way people were feeling locally, perhaps "mollicate" would have been a better word in verse 5!

4 — The official Dundee FC programme (1983) lists 20 December 1898 as the date on which the present club was founded. This was indeed the date on which the committee which was ultimately to give the club continuity was elected but, given that these same men had by and large been instrumental in founding the club in 1893, it is a date in the summer of that year which I believe should be the official oine, either the date of the

formal discussions between Our Boys and East End (20 May), the date of admission to the Scottish League (12 June), or the date of the election of the first Dundee committee (20 June). Furthermore, the new committe of 1898 was quoted at the time by the most reputable sports journal in the country, *Scottish Sport*, as wishing to make the club "not a new body, but merely a reorganised continuation". The Directors of the Dundee Football Club at the turn of the century were:

J Robertson (Chairman) (Stair Railer)

A Williamson (VC) (Mechanic)

G Walker (Machinist)

A Spalding (Joiner)

J Cameron (Collector)

and shares here also held by D MacLennan (Traveller) and W Wallace (Clerk), who was also Secretary/Manager.

5

IF ANY DISCERNIBLE pattern can be said to exist in the city's footballing history, it is that when one team has been enjoying success, the other (or others, as it was in earlier days) has tended to suffer a relative decline. I am not suggesting that this is some kind of immutable law, that the future is fixed; indeed, I look forward to the time when the pattern is broken, but to date, Dundee has never had more than one team enjoying success at any given time — although a case could be argued that if one club is enjoying *major* success this serves as a spur to the other to get down to some hard work and longer-term planning.

At the turn of the century, Dundee FC were shaping up for glory. Although Wanderers won the Northern League in 1899-1900 the Dark Blues[1] reigned supreme in the town, and when Dens Park was opened on 19 August 1899 they had an impressive stadium to match their First Division status.

The club appeared to have put their financial troubles behind them and under their first manager/secretary, William Wallace, proceeded to enjoy ten years of comparative success. In an eighteen-club First Division they were runners-up three times, 1902-03, 1906-07 and 1908-09, on the third occasion losing the championship by only one point to Celtic and thus firmly establishing themselves as the most consistent "provincial" club in the country. A number of their players were also capped by Scotland — William Muir, John Fraser, Peter Robertson, James Sharp, George Chaplin, Alex MacFarlane and John "Sailor" Hunter. Sharp went on to play for Rangers, Fulham and Arsenal and has been described by the English press as "a renowned defender of the Edwardian era" but it was the Sailor — so called for his rolling gait — and his teammates who would achieve immortality.

Remembering the better times with Jack Hillman, Dundee FC developed something of a partiality towards English League players and at least six of the 1909-10 team were brought to the club from England by Peter Allan, the scout who had earlier acquired the reputation of robbing local clubs of their best players. Herbert Dainty came from New Brighton; Jack Fraser and Alex MacFarlane from Newcastle United; Bert Lee from Southampton; Sailor Hunter from Portsmouth; and Jimmy Bellamy from Woolwich Arsenal via Portsmouth. They, along with Crumley, Neal, MacEwan, Comrie and "Puddin" Langlands, comprised the team which embarked upon the new season.

Their league performance was not quite up to the standard of the previous year, but a record crowd of 29,000 had attended a Cup-tie with Rangers at Dens Park in 1909 and the 1910 campaign could not come quickly enough. In the first round the club drew minor opposition in the shape of Beith (away) but as was the custom, the bigger club purchased the ground rights. It still took two games, however, both played at Dens Park (1-1, 1-0) to account for the Ayrshire men. In the second round Dundee were at home to Falkirk, who were second top of the First Division, but they were more easily dealt with (3-0), and before a record attendance at Fir Park, they then dismissed Motherwell, by three goals to one.

In the semi-final Dundee met the Edinburgh Hibs, a top-class team. It was not until the third game, played at Celtic Park, that they secured a 1-0 victory with Hunter getting the winner (the first two games resulted in 0-0 draws) to take them to a Final against Clyde. The Blues now genuinely believed they had a great chance, for Clyde had provided a remarkable series of shocks in the tournament, defeating Rangers, Queen's Park and Celtic in earlier rounds. With great anticipation, the Dundee fans made their way to Ibrox Park on 9 April 1910. In all, some 50,000 people attended this match and an outstanding game resulted in a 2-2 draw, Langlands, with the last kick of the match and Robertson (o.g.) equalising two first half goals by Clyde. This meant a replay and again the match was drawn, 0-0, but the *Daily Record* gave Dundee the "artistic" edge in the second game, so by the time the third game came around, the pendulum of favour was definitely swinging from west to east.

On Wednesday 20 April 1910, the Scottish Cup came to the city of

Dundee FC 1910 Scottish Cup Winners.
Back Row: J Dundas (Linesman), B Neal, R McEwan, G Comrie, W Wallace,
(Secretary and Manager), H Dainty, J Chaplin, R Crumley,
W Longair (Trainer).
Sitting; A Hall, J Hunter, G Langlands, A Lee (Capt), A MacFarlane,
J Lawson, J Fraser.
Front Row: J Bellamy and D McCann.

(Courtesy: DC Thomson)

Dundee for the first (and, to date, the only) time. The famous team was: Crumley; Neal and MacEwan; Lee, Dainty and Comrie; Bellamy, Langlands, Hunter, MacFarlane and Fraser.

Chalmers opened the scoring for Clyde in three minutes but the Clyde captain then made the tactical error of dropping back instead of pressing home the advantage and when Bellamy equalised with a header before half-time, the Dundee hopes were high. In the second-half it was their fitness which commentators believed gave the edge, for it had been a bad winter and all three games had been played in heavy conditions. It was therefore fitting that the training of former stalwart "Plum" Longair should play its part in the club's first real moment of triumph. Late in the match, with some Dundee supporters having left early in anticipation of another draw, Hunter took advantage of a blunder by two Clyde defenders and shot over the shoulder of the goalkeeper and into the net. "Thus cups are won and

45

lost," said the *Record*.

Lee, Dainty and Fraser were the men of the moment, having performed superbly in all three games, and an emotional Bailie Robertson, in accepting the trophy could only find enough words to say that it was the height of the club's ambition to win the Scottish Cup. The team was cheered off by several thousand at Buchanan Street station; cheered again by large numbers at Perth; and when they arrived at the old West Station at 11 o'clock that night, between fifteen and twenty thousand people awaited them. Horses were taken from a brake (carriage) and all the players and officials were pulled in triumphant procession through the main streets,[2] culminating in supper at the Royal British Hotel. It was the early hours of the morning before the town quietened down. The players' bonus, it was thought, would reach "double figures" (£10 or £15)[3] and with public subscription might rise to £30, a lot of money when one considers that most agricultural labourers earned less than £1 a week at the time.

The press reaction locally, however, was somewhat muted the next day. Although the *Courier* reported that cheering crowds had fought for the special edition of the *Evening Telegraph* earlier in the night (something which can't have happened too often), its editorial was bland and extreme and even the *Advertiser*, 109 years old and described on its centenary by the *Record* has having been a "strong liberal organ when liberalism was unfashionable and its advocates propagators of sedition", even the "radical" *Advertiser* found space to bemoan the fact that the cup was "won to a large extent by Southerners".

NOTES

1 — Dark blue jerseys were not officially adopted by the club until 1902. From 1893-96 they alternated between the dark blue of Our Boys and the blue and white stripes of East End, and from 1896-1902 they played in what became the "alternative" Dundee stip of white shirts and black shorts.

2 — The Brake actually collapsed in Victoria Road and the players had to complete the journey to Dens Park on foot.

3 — Cup Final Teams:
1st Game: Crumley; Lawson and Chaplin; Lee, Dainty and Comrie; Bellamy, Langlands, Hunter, MacFarlane and Fraser.
2nd Game: Neal replaced Lawson.
3rd Game: MacEwan replaced Chaplin.

6

DUNDEE FC'S SCOTTISH CUP victory was rightly hailed as a fine achievement by everyone interested in football but it was far from the case that all the other clubs in the town had given up hope of emulating their success. Certainly, Harp had lost the initiative by regularly going in and out of business, but Wanderers and the still-amateur Lochee United (the "Queen's Park of the North") had both battled into the twentieth century and it was not only the Dundee patrons who were grateful for this. Many commentators remarked around the time that had it not been for the hard work of the officials of these clubs, not only the Forfarshire but, indeed, the Aberdeen Clubs — Victoria United, Orion and Aberdeen — would have been isolated and in great difficulty. Perhaps recognising this fact, the three Aberdeen teams decided to follow the Dundee FC example and amalgamate as Aberdeen Football Club. In 1903 the new grouping took up residence at Pittodrie — a Celtic word meaning "dung-heap"!

The Dundee soil, however, did not prove so fertile for Lochee United and Wanderers. By season 1907-08, both clubs were anchored at the foot of the Northern League which by then had also incorporated some Fife teams, and following their deposition at St Margarets Park by Harp Juniors,[1] Lochee United failed to compete in the 1908-09 League. A new ground was eventually found by the club (also in Lochee) but Wanderers were not so lucky.

Following another poor season (1908-09) their lease of Clepington Park became due. Now, whether more money was offered is uncertain, but the Wanderers were suddenly shocked to learn that a Mr Pat Reilly, secretary of the newly-formed Dundee Hibs, had approached the Clepington landlord over the heads of the Wanderers to secure the lease and thereby evict them from the ground which had been their home, almost without interruption, for some nineteen years. This proved to be a virtual death blow to the Wanderers for although they managed to turn in some creditable performances over the next few years, particularly in view of the fact they had no permanent home, they never recovered the lost ground, so to speak, and went out of business at the onset of the First World War. Their magnificent efforts, however, in endeavouring to rival the more powerful Dundee amalgamation and, even more important, in identifying and consolidating the Clepington area as the natural "home of football" in the town should not, and indeed did not, go unrecognised.

What was this organisation, the new Dundee Hibs, and where had they come from? The *People's Journal,* believe it or not, was at this time a fairly radical sister-paper to the *Dundee Advertiser* and as such, in touch with the Irish community in the town. On 20 March 1909 it recorded the following:

> For some time there has been talk in the city with regard to the formation of a new Irish senior team and a committee at the head of which is Mr P Reilly, cycle dealer, is working at the business. Of course everyone wants to see a return of the days when the old Harp was a power in the land, but it is much to be feared our enthusiastic friends scarcely know the magnitude of the task they have undertaken in these altered times. Meanwhile the plan is to secure a ground in the *east end*[2] of the city (my italics), one being in view, and also to seek admission to the Northern League, which should be easily gained in view of recent developments, for St Johnstone and Arbroath have decided to follow the Fife clubs into the new Central League. As to players the Committee is pleasingly optimistic, and friends of the game will wish them well in their endeavour to restore the lost prestige of Irish football in the city. It will be an uphill task but perseverance, enthusiasm and — money, may accomplish much.[3]

Dundee Hibs, therefore, were founded sometime in the second half of March 1909. It was obviously not their original intention to dispossess the Wanderers of Clepington Park and when it was announced (on 17 April) that they had done so, it was not the morality but the wisdom of such a move which was questioned by the *Journal.* "It is the proximity to Dens Park," said their correspondent, "which has been the undoing of the Wanderers who, if they can manage to get a ground in another quarter of the city will be well out of Clepington." Or on 1 May: "The Wanderers have got notice to quit so that the *nice little tangle* has got beyond controversy and the public now knows how matters stand. The new Hibs mean to do big things and it is hoped they will be successful, but they have certainly made a very big initial blunder in going to Clepington Park *which has been a starvation hole from first to last"*. (my italics)

Pat Reilly and Tom Timmons.
Principal founders of Dundee Hibs 1909.

(Courtesy: *Catholic Herald*)

A "nice little tangle" it certainly was and, like the Harp before them, it was noted on Hibs' record by the footballing fraternity. The "Forkies" were particularly embittered and although instructed by a lawyer to leave the fittings of Clepington Park they ignored him and sold them to a "wrecker", stipulating that he was to remove everything from the field. Hibs offered him £20 profit on his transaction to allow the erections to stand but Wanderers would not listen and even removed the fence which, as Dundee FC player Sandy MacFarlane noted at the time, left Clepington Park "bare as a bald head".

Whatever their initial difficulties, however, Dundee Hibs, in keeping with their Glasgow counterparts, appear to have found a great enthusiast and legislator in Pat Reilly. Reilly (born 1874) had come from Ireland as a child with his parents and entered the cycle trade at the age of eighteen, opening a shop on the south side of Perth Road. The business prospered when women took up cycling and he then opened branches in Leith, Perth and Edinburgh, where he developed a keen interest in the fortunes of Edinburgh Hibs.

This association then fired him to establish a similar club in Dundee (a senior Irish club Erin Rovers FC was also established in Perth in 1909) and with the support of Tom Timmons, T Malone, John Naulty, James Glover, J Hennessy and ex-Provost Hawick of Forfar (Wallace the baker also had a financial interest) he founded the Dundee Hibs. Reilly was active in Liberal politics and church business but the new club, whilst acknowledging the importance of the Catholic church in the community at large, appear to have decided not to have clergymen *directly* involved in the running of their affairs, and were never sectarian in their choice of players.

They played in green jerseys and white shorts and on Tuesday 25 May 1909, were admitted to the SFA. The Dundee papers did not report this in spite of the fact that the Hibs had been pressed by the SFA to produce evidence that they had indeed taken over the tenancy of Clepington Park, but on 1 June they did mention that at a meeting of the Scottish League the previous night, Dundee Hibs, by obtaining only three votes in a ballot, had failed to gain admission to the Second Division. The Hibs were undeterred, however, and on 18 August 1909, in front of 7,000 fans, they inaugurated Tannadice Park (which Clepington Park had been renamed) with a match against their Edinburgh namesakes. It was a gala occasion and memories of the old Harp were revived[4] when the Very Rev Provost Holder congratulated the directors on their fine team. The band from the *Mars* training ship played and Dundee Hibs lined up: Brady (from Lochgelly United); Hannan (St Johnstone) and Gallacher (Wanderers); Strachan (St Josephs), Ramsay (Brechin City) and Boland (St Josephs); Flood (Dundee A), McDermott, Docherty (both Forfar), Dailly (Dundee A) and Brown (Kirkcaldy United). In a 1-1 draw, the Edinburgh Hibs player who scored the first goal of the match won a bicycle, and it was Docherty who equalised. The following week the wolf lay down with the lamb when the aggrieved Wanderers returned to Tannadice, but for once it was the lamb who knocked it off, Wanderers winning 2-1.

Dundee Hibs' first victory came on 28 August when, in front of a handsome gate, they defeated Montrose 1-0, although the first local derby between them and Dundee resulted in a 3-0 victory for the Dundee (A) team. The Hibs did much better in the next match (February 1910) however, when a narrow 1-2 defeat at the hands of the Scottish Cup heroes served to raise a few eyebrows in the town. The club was now determined to make its presence felt in any way possible. On 9 April they flew in the face of tradition by arranging an away game against St Mirren at Paisley when Dundee were playing their first Cup Final seven miles along the road at Ibrox. With another piece of monumental opportunism they arranged to play Clyde at Tannadice two days after the final! Reilly's tactics obviously worked, however, following some canvassing and the distribution of a circular in May 1910 in which he informed the other Scottish clubs that: the Hibs had spent £3,000 on Tannadice and were now clear of debt; the Pavilion was two storeys high and built of brick; the dressing rooms were fitted up in the latest style, with cold and hot water baths; the stand could take 1,200 people and the ground 15-20,000; the club's inclusion in the Second Division would gratify the city's 50,000 Irish population and open up interest in that League. Following this public relations exercise he secured their admission to the Second Division on 7 June 1910.

Neither the Northern League nor the East Coast Carrie Cup was completed that year, but both tournaments gave the club useful experience and when Second Division football returned to Tannadice after almost sixteen years, the Hibs were ready for it. The first two

PROBABLE QUALIFYING CUP FINALISTS.

Dundee Hibs Qualifying Cup Finalists 1913.
Back Row: M Fox (Trainer), G Forbes, C M'Phillips, W Welsh, E M'Donald,
D Martin, J Hannan.
Front Row: J Govan, P Currie, W Henderson, T Boland, F Leckie,
F Stoessell. Inset P Reilly (Manager).
(Courtesy: *Peoples Journal*, Dundee City Library)

matches against Leith and East Stirling were lost but a 4-1 victory over Abercorn on 17 September was followed by three draws and three wins and, following some heady days near the top of the League, they finished a creditable ninth in their first season.

Dundee FC meanwhile finished fourth in the First Division and gave a stout defence of the Cup, reaching the semi-final in which they lost 3-2 to Hamilton Accies — and the city also experienced the excitement of a General Election (December 1910) in which one of the MPs elected for Dundee was none other than Winston Churchill. Churchill, who was a Liberal at this time, had first been elected to represent Dundee at a by-election in 1908 and confidently expected to hold the seat for the rest of his life. Dundee folk, however, are not as green as they're cabbage-looking.

The high-water mark in the history of Dundee Hibs was reached in season 1913-14. The Hibs were early exponents of a local scouting system and their first team which by then consisted of nine locals — a record for a First or Second Division club — was in with a chance of going into the First Division as there was talk of increasing the number of clubs to twenty (there was no promotion at this time, but the club had had a good season).

Promotion did not, in fact, materialise, but the Hibs were not to be denied their moment of glory and it came in the Qualifying Cup. This was a lesser tournament than the Scottish Cup, obviously, but fiercely contested nevertheless by Second Division and other senior clubs. The early results were as follows: First Round, Hibs 2 Brechin City 0; Second Round, Hibs 3 Dunfermline 0; Third Round, a bye; and Fourth Round, 2-1 at home to East Stirling, following a 1-1 away draw. The Fifth Round game with Forfar at Tannadice was the "talk of the town and country" and Reilly was indignant at suggestions that the club might ask for the use of Dens Park to accommodate the anticipated 15-20,000 crowd. In the event Tannadice was improved for the game which was won 1-0. Hibs were now unbeaten for a year at home in League and Cup games but they were taken to a replay in the semi-final by Inverness Caley. 500 fans made the journey and witnessed a 2-0 victory in the Highland capital.

On Saturday, 13 December 1913, they met Albion Rovers in the final at Tynecastle. The Dundee Hibs team was: McPhillips; Hannan and Forbes; White, Henderson and Boland; Brown, E MacDonald, Martin, Linn and Stoessel. The first game was drawn 1-1 (Brown) and so was the second, 0-0 at Easter Road, and these were good performances from the Hibs team who lagged behind the Whifflet team in the League. On Saturday 27 December they returned to Tynecastle only to lose 3-0 but, all things considered, the future was not looking altogether unpromising for the Tannadice Hibs when the nation received the news on 4 August 1914, that Britain was at war with Germany.

NOTES

1 — Harp (seniors) collapsed in 1897 partly because they could not find a permanent home. Harp (juniors) began in 1904 and they, too, were without a home until they replaced Lochee United at St Margaret's Park (Gardner Street/Kilberry Street) whence they became known as Lochee Harp. They were therefore different clubs but from the same tradition, and their strips and club badges were identical.

2 — The *Evening Telegraph* reported that the club had tried to find a ground in the *west end*. The *Catholic Herald* said two sites were under review.

3 — The *Catholic Herald* (27/3/09) also said.
". . . Dundee Hibernians are now a duly organised body . . . The promoters are all Dundee Irishmen, and as the city is said to include in its population no less than 30,000 of the same persuasion, the new organisation will not want support. Mr P Reilly . . . has been appointed secretary. The new club is meant to take the place of the defunct Harp."

4 — Paddy Rock, formerly of Dundee Harp, hoisted the green flag over Tannadice at the inaugural game.

7

ALTHOUGH BOTH Dundee FC and Dundee Hibs maintained teams throughout the First World War football obviously became something of an irrelevance. The "B" Division was suspended and at one point both Dundee FC and Aberdeen were asked to stand down from the First Division to minimise travelling. On the resumption of the First Division proper in 1919, however, Dundee FC, with former player Sandy MacFarlane installed as manager (Dundee's first full-time paid official) and William McIntosh as Chairman, went on to build some of their best-ever sides which, although they did not win anything, reached the final of the Scottish Cup in 1925 and contained a number of outstanding individuals. There was goalkeeper Willie Fotheringham; "iron-men" Dyken Nicoll and Willie Rankine; David "Napper" Thomson, a full-back and capped against Wales; Davie Raitt, also a full-back and great character who was transferred to Everton in 1922 but later returned to the city; Davie Halliday, a prolific goalscorer who came originally from Dumfries and who held the club record until the 1940s (38 goals in one season); and Alec Troup, the first Dundee FC player to be capped against England and who would undoubtedly have received more honours but for the fact he played in the same left-wing position as the "Wee Blue Devil", Alan Morton of Rangers. Troup was also transferred to Everton, in 1923.

The post-war Dundee FC management showed great enterprise in buying Dens Park in 1919 for £5,000 and by the time the ground had been renovated and a new grandstand built in 1921 (the one which remains today)[1] the club was said to have spent some £60,000. This meant a new issue of capital, but contrary to the expectations and

Dundee Hibs August 1923.
Back Row: W Hutchison (Director), D Simpson (Director), Richards,
Brownlie, O'Kane, A Lamb (Director), Robertson (Trainer),
W Hogg (Director).
Sitting: Gilmour, Kay, Porter, Hannah, J Dickson (Director).
Kneeling: McEwan, Knox, Cottingham, Stirling.
The Club became Dundee United on 17 October 1923.

(Courtesy: DC Thomson)

desire of many of the supporters, the club decided to remain a private company with approximately thirty new shareholders joining the existing twenty or so and the Directorial shareholding increased from twenty-five to two hundred.

Dundee Hibs were just as ambitious but neither as rich nor as successful as their neighbours. In season 1919-20 they competed in and won the Eastern League with a side which contained a number of ex-Dundee players. The usual pool was J Crumley (later transferred to Swansea), Mulholland, Henderson, D S Miller, Wilson, Herron, Hughes, Bradley, Gibson, Cargill, F Murray and Wilkie, and Pat Reilly remained in charge. In season 1920-21 the club moved into the Central League, and improvements were made to the pavilion and dressing rooms, but this was all in preparation for the return to the Second Division to which they were admitted on its restart in 1921.

"We are on the eve of the greatest season in the club's history," said one unnamed official and it was just as well he was unnamed, for his judgement was somewhat wide of the mark. In a disastrous season from a playing point of view, the club sank to second bottom of the League and, since 1921-22 was to be the first which led to automatic promotion and relegation, Dundee Hibs were dropped from the "B" Division along with Clackmannan.

1921-22 was a difficult time throughout Europe with post-war unemployment causing riots, and in Dundee the soup kitchen at Constable Street baths was serving up to 1,000 people per day. 1921-22, however, also marked a significant political development in Britain and one which was to conspire with the evil of unemployment to cast an even darker shadow over Tannadice — for this was the time of the Ulster Treaty which, instigated by Lloyd George and supported by Winston Churchill, separated the six counties of Ulster from the twenty-six of the Irish Free State. Now, public opinion about Ireland had changed dramatically following the Easter Rebellion of 1916, and when the violence was stepped up in Britain after the War (indeed some Irish political prisoners were jailed at Perth) the position of a poor and lowly-placed club with Irish connections would have become precarious indeed.

And it was not as though the local press handled the issue, or the clubs for matter, with equanimity. Even allowing for the fact that Dundee FC were the more successful of the two, the Hibs' achievements prior to the War merited encouragement and considerably more than the occasional acknowledgement given to them by the so-called "liberal" *Advertiser*. D C Thomson's *Courier* and *Evening Telegraph* were often even greater offenders in this respect. When Hibs were dropped from the Second Division the *Courier*, whose leading sports writer went by the unambiguous pseudonym of "Dark Blue", devoted more space to the plight of Queen's Park who faced automatic relegation to the Second Division than to the plight of the Dundee Hibs, who faced extinction.

Fortunately this bias was countered at an official level in the person of Willie Maley and when the Hibs announced their impending demise to the Scottish League on 28 June 1922, the club was assisted in the same way as Dundee FC had been in 1898. By what now might be called the "Tayside Solution", players' registrations and transfer rights were held by the League to whom the clubs were requested to make offers, one-third of which the League would retain. And as the Hibs also indicated a willingness to soldier on with a reconstructed board, a place was eventually found for them in the Alliance League which was the province of the reserve teams of First Division clubs.

In this new situation help was forthcoming from a number of sources, but none more unusual than the whimsically-named UNOMI, football correspondent of the *People's Journal*. As I said earlier, the *Journal* remained fairly true to its historical liberal principles following John Leng's decision to bring his publications under DC Thomson's umbrella and as late as the 1920s its football correspondent held a remarkably independent line.

First of all he welcomed the proposed reconstruction of the Hibs' board. Reilly and his men had done a fine job and would retain an interest in the club, but a new challenge was now to be faced and the prospect of a new board of local businessmen buying out the old company and floating a new one seemed to UNOMI to be the correct path. The new Chairman was James Dickson, and his principal directors William Hutchison, William Hogg, William Burke Jun., and David Simpson. A club manager was also appointed in December 1922, one Peter O'Rourke, who had previously managed Bradford (although he lasted only four months).

At this point UNOMI entered the annals of the club's history. Following a 1st round Scottish Cup Hibs victory over Beith, the journalist fell into conversation with some friends who, like himself, were puzzled as to why this reasonably attractive match should pull only some 3,000 people, one quarter of the attendance at Dens Park the same day where Dundee FC met the "minnows", Vale of Atholl. What emerged from that conversation was of great significance to the Tannadice club for in his next article (20 January 1923) UNOMI put forward the suggestion that Dundee Hibs change their name. "No tradition attaches to the Dundee Hibs," he said, except one "associated with misfortune". Indeed the name was "A barrier which keeps many from giving personal practical support to the club" and, reading between the lines, there is no doubt that what everyone was talking abut was the Irish connotations of the name. The article created a sensation in local football circles, or at least so UNOMI said, and his headline the next week ran *"People's Journal* Tip Adopted". Underneath he revealed that the club were to take up his suggestion, keeping the name Dundee Hibs until after their application to rejoin the League was considered, then changing it to DUNDEE CITY.

By May 1923 the representations had been made and, at the expense of East Stirling, Hibs returned to the "B" Division with Arbroath. It was later revealed that William McIntosh, the Dundee FC's influential representative on the League Committee, had opposed Hibs' return on the grounds that he did not think the city of Dundee could maintain two First League clubs. William Hutchison naturally disagreed and personally thanked the *People's Journal* for their support.

Not everyone, of course, was absorbed by the idiosyncrasies of football and, at least in Dundee, Buffalo Bill was still alive. Well, actually, he was dead but his memory and that of the Wild West lingered on, for in the summer of 1922 none other than "Young Buffalo" (who?) was billed to appear at the Kings Theatre (later the Gaumont Cinema and now the County Bingo). The show was apparently a "romance" which featured "real Red Indians" and a horse which a reviewer said "could do everything but speak". That made a change. In the more credulous 1890s the *Advertiser* carried a piece about a donkey in America which, it was reported, actually could speak! And on a more serious note Dundee's jute workers became embroiled in a strike which began in February 1923 and, in the case of the Lochee workers, lasted for twenty-seven weeks, including two periods of lockout.

On 29 May 1923, Dundee Hibs appointed Jimmy Brownlie, the famous Third Lanark goalkeeper, player-manager of the club. Brownlie had won a number of caps for Scotland between 1909 and 1914 and his arrival marked the beginning of a new era in Dundee football. Alexander Lamb replaced Burke on the Hibs board and at an AGM on 20 August 1923 the club formally decided to change their name to Dundee City. The *Courier* had also predicted that the name would be changed as "The Irish element in the management of the club has practically been eliminated" and although the choice of words was perhaps unfortunate, of the new board members only Simpson had any connection with the old Hibs club and he would only last until 1925 — all of which reinforces the belief that there was a definite move afoot to play down the "Irishness" of the new club.

Applications were now put forward to the SFA and the Board of Trade in respect of the Dundee City Athletic Association. The Register of Joint Stock Companies finally sanctioned the Dundee City Athletic *Club* Ltd, but the letter to the SFA only arrived one day before their meeting on 19 September 1923 (shades of Dundee County, Harp and Dundonians) and once again Dundee FC protested, this time on the rather curious grounds that there was a possibility of "confusion of correspondence". Further, it was not in their (Dundee FC's) interest "to have another club bearing the principal part of their name (Dundee) in such a similar title". UNOMI immediately sprang to the defence of common sense, and the Hibs. "I wonder," he asked rhetorically, "how the Sheffield clubs manage; also the two Manchester combines and the rival organisations of Bristol and Bradford?" UNOMI also criticised Dundee FC's delay in making their protest, and given that the Companies Register had passed the name, asked what price a legal argument?

Dundee FC 1924.
Back Row: Thomson, Rankine, Halliday, Britton, Nicholson, McNab.
Front Row: Irving, McLean, Ross, Duncan, McDonald.
(Courtesy: DC Thomson)

Dundee FC were simply "getting the breeze up" remarked one newspaper letter-writer, but following some discussion the casting vote of Chairman T White of Celtic went against the Hibs' proposal. Two members of the SFA Committee, however, whose votes would have given Hibs the change they sought had to leave early (one actually missed his train into the bargain) and so on 17 October 1923, the Tannadice directors tried again. No comments were forthcoming at this meeting so the letter was allowed to lie on the table whilst the clubs conferred outside. There it was "agreeably entertained that the name of Dundee Hibernians FC be changed to Dundee United". Dundee FC were represented by McIntosh who apparently only objected to the name Dundee City, whilst the Hibs' men, Hutchison, Hogg and Brownlie, were willing to adopt any name "so long as the word 'Hibs' went out". McIntosh then returned to the meeting and placed the proposal before the President, saying Dundee FC would support it.[2]

"The bond of friendship," said the *Journal*, "has been sealed between the clubs and nothing but harmony (*sic*) will prevail in future. In fact, there may be quite a lot of 'come and go' between the respective officials and this, I think, should be for their mutual benefit". Just how much "come and go" would actually take place no-one, least of all William McIntosh, could have foreseen.

In their first game as Dundee United, played against Kings Park of Stirling on 20 October 1923, the Tannadice team beat the Second Division leaders by three goals to two[3] away from home. They lined up: Brownlie; Kay and Stirling; Swan, Richards and Porter; McEwan, Cottingham, O'Kane, Mackie and Gilmour, with Gilfeather as reserve, and their colours, white shirts and white shorts (the intended black shorts did not materialise for this game) earned them their first nickname, the "Bakers".[4]

To summarise, therefore, Dundee United suffered a longer period of gestation than Dundee FC and in some ways it was a more complicated birth. Although not the result of an amalgamation in the final analysis they were nevertheless the result of a fusion of ideals which ultimately could only prosper if the positive qualities of the Wanderers (a *friendly* "Scottish" Club with good staying power) were allied to those of the Hibs or Harp (at times *dynamic* "Irish" organisations, due mainly to the personal commitment and drive of their best-known officials) in an organisation dedicated to good football of a non-sectarian character.

In many ways the appointment of Jimmy Brownlie — a respected professional and a Protestant — provided the link, almost in the same way that many years later, a man with similar "credentials" would galvanise another Scottish club with Irish connections.

NOTES
1 — The original grandstand brought from Carolina Port, was on the opposite side of Dens Park and burned down in 1921. In his autobiography *Soccer Rebel*, Jimmy

Guthrie hints at the insurance implications.

2 — The *Catholic Herald* by this time had apparently given up on the Hibs, as none of this was reported.

3 — United's goalscorers were Mackie (2) and Gilmour, Mackie scoring Dundee United's first.

4 — Dundee FC's first nickname was the "Sugar Bags" as dark blue and white were the colours of the sugar bags made in the Dundee Mills.

8

THIS, THEN, WAS the "Roaring Twenties". Jack Dempsey was heavy-weight champion of the world. Rudyard Kipling replaced JM Barrie as Rector of St Andrews University and at the General Election of 1923 Dundee once again returned the Prohibitionist, Neddy Scrymgeour, who had caused a sensation the previous year by ousting Winston Churchill as one of Dundee's two MPs.[1] No party was strong enough on its own to form a government but with the support of the Liberals, the Labour Party came to power for the first time on 21 January 1924, and with Scot Ramsay MacDonald as Prime Minister.

The *Daily Record's* election editorial had struck what was to become a familiar tabloid chord by exhorting the Liberals "not to open the door to Labour extremists by rejecting a coalition with the Tories" and its sports pages also had a familiar ring. Dundee FC's failure to seriously challenge, it contended, could be attributed to the fact that the club's good scouting system was continuously negated by a willingness to transfer star players. A successful United, it contended, would also help Dundee — although what would help United it did not say.

In Season 1923-24 United finished ninth and Dundee FC fifth in their respective Divisions, but 1924-25 was to be a better one for the clubs. United, who by this time had adopted the black and white colours, topped the Second Division after seven games and maintained an unbeaten away record until the end of November. Dundee's League form that season was not so convincing and on 24 December 1924 with the club lying twelfth, their manager, Sandy MacFarlane, resigned. The directors decided not to replace him right away but to look after the team themselves and it paid off to some extent for in the Scottish Cup Dundee FC once again found form.

In the first round they defeated Johnstone 5-0 while United beat Aberdeen University 5-1. In the second round the Tannadice team went down 5-1 to Partick Thistle (away) but Dundee beat Lochgelly United 2-1, and in the third round managed to account for the Cup-holders Airdrie, by three goals to one. In the fourth round Broxburn United were despatched by one goal to nil at Dens and in a semi-final replay Hamilton Accies went the same way, by two goals to nil. United, meanwhile, were still enjoying *their* success in League football and continued to top the Second Division with the following side: Bridgeford; Kay and Osborne; Harvey, MacRoberts and Gilfeather; Simpson, Oswald, Collins, Bauld and Gilmour.

Dundee FC, however, had their sights on "higher" things and on 11 April 1925, in front of a 75,000 crowd, they met Celtic in the Scottish Cup Final. Dundee FC lined up as follows: Britton; Brown and Thomson; Ross, W Rankine and Irving;[2] Duncan, McLean, Halliday, J Rankine and Gilmour. The Celtic team included two McStays, Patsy Gallacher and the young Jimmy McGrory, and the crowd was the second largest ever to have attended a Scottish Cup Final. A number of special trains travelled from Dundee. Inside-right McLean (Davie, not Jim) opened the scoring for the Dark Blues after half an hour and this was the only goal of the first half. In the 26th minute of the second half, though, something remarkable happened. Following a free-kick, Patsy Gallacher collected and weaved towards the Dundee goal-line where the ball became lodged between his feet. Thinking quickly, instead of trying to release it, he simply "tumbled over his wilkies" (no relation) thus throwing himself into the goal — and the history books. Four minutes from time McGrory made it two and the Dundee support were forced to make that familiar and depressing journey home.

Davie Halliday, who had come to Dens via QOS and St Mirren, was soon after transferred to Sunderland (for £4,000) to replace the legendary Charlie Buchan who was en route to Arsenal and his own magazine. Halliday was another who would have had more international recognition but for the excellence of the competition (Hughie Gallacher, McGrory), although he did get into the record books by scoring 100 goals in 101 games in the English First Division and in all scored 221 goals in 400 League and Cup games. His goalscoring equal would not be seen in a dark blue jersey for another twenty years.

On the same day as the 1925 Cup Final United secured promotion by beating East Stirling and on 18 April they won the Second Division Championship following a draw with Broxburn. Their record was Played 38, Won 20, Lost 8, Drawn 10, Goals for 58, Against 44, Points 50. Jimmy Brownlie's achievements were, therefore, quite remarkable in giving the city its second First Division club so soon and it was generally thought that when one or two positions were strengthened and fitness attained, United would develop into a good side.

On May Day 1925, Dundee City Athletic Club, formerly called Dundee Hibernian Football and Athletic Company Ltd, sold all "business, property and assets, fixtures, fittings, erections and utensils" to the newly-incorporated Dundee United Football Company Ltd. The price was 1,966 shares at £1 (which went mainly to the Reilly family) and payment of debts not exceeding £4,810.

In total, the Dundee United Football Company hoped to sell 2,500 shares at £1 but, initially, demand was slight. The Directors, Hutchison, Dickson, Hogg, Lamb, Simpson and David Godfrey pressed on regardless, buying Tannadice Park for £2,500 and issuing Debentures of £4,050 at 5% in cash with the ground used as security. The plan was that the whole income of the stand and half of the income of a projected new stand would be paid to the trustees in redemption of the debentures and interest. The Tannadice pitch was also to be levelled, drained and shifted west.

As was customary with a club entering the First Division for the first time, a League delegation headed by Willie Maley visited Tannadice and appeared to be favourably impressed by what they saw and heard. Once again, UNOMI was on the spot to record events for posterity and in a classic piece of journalistic enterprise he passed the following information on to his readers (30 May 1924): "Prospectuses of the new company will be out next week. It is hoped the public will take an interest in the matter. *The officials want the club to be the People's club."* (my italics)

' On 14 August 1925 United signed a strong young forward named Jimmy Simpson[3] from Newburgh West End and in their First Division match they lined up: Paterson; Kay and McBride; Campbell, D Walker and J Walker; T Simpson, Bauld, J Simpson, Howieson and J McDonald. The match against Raith Rovers (away) was lost 4-2 (Howieson 2) but a victory was soon achieved against St Johnstone and on 19 September they astonished the Scottish footballing public by beating Celtic 1-0 at Tannadice and going above Dundee in the League. They then proceeded to slump badly, however, and after eleven games, were in bottom position. The first First Division derby match was played at Dens Park on 21 November 1925. The score was 0-0 and United were thought to have just as many fans as their neighbours. "Plum" Longair described the result as "a grand away result for United", but Glasgow's *Daily Record* continued in the traditional tone of patronisation. "Jack is as good as his master," said the columnist. United actually finished the season seventeenth with Dundee (now managed by ex-Celt, Alec McNair) tenth out of twenty.

And so the twenties roared on. The admission price for football was still sixpence and a crowd of 100,000 was recorded for an Old Firm match. Silent cinema was at its peak with Rudolf Valentino one of its great stars, although "talkies" were on the way and both would suffer competition from what was to become another pastime — popular dancing. Late night dancing was in fact banned at this time in South Wales where it was described by its detractors as "dangerous excitement" and a "sensuous menace" and such over-reaction was probably due to concern about the general increase in social unrest which had developed in the so-called "land fit for heroes" in the years following the First World War. Things came to a head on 3 May 1926 when a dispute between the National Union of Mineworkers and the coalowners (mines were in private hands at this time) escalated into a General Strike. The general action lasted less than two weeks, as the TUC had not been properly prepared for such a conflict but the miners, faced with increased working hours or reduced wages, stayed out for some six months, and individuals faced starvation in many cases. In Fife (and South Wales) their solidarity was particularly strong, but it was giving way elsewhere and following arbitration (by church bishops) they came to accept defeat.

In Dundee, the General Strike temporarily closed down both the *Advertiser* and the *Courier* and in a surprise development the heirs of John Leng, the distinguished proprietor of the *Advertiser* transferred the controlling interest in that newspaper to David Couper Thomson, who had been his opposite number at the *Courier*.[4] The move was surprising because the *Courier* had been established in 1816 as the organ of Tory interest to combat the Liberal influence of the *Advertiser* (founded 1801) and Thomson had never shown the slightest sympathy for Liberalism. Having gained the effective press monopoly, however (for the Dundee businessmen who provided the essential advertising revenue had no interest in a Labour alternative — the *Dundee Free Press*), Thomson now relentlessly pursued an anti-Trade Union policy amongst his workers and was able to intensify the promotion of his parochial Tory viewpoint by virtue of the monopoly position. This would prove to be another factor in the shaping of the Dundee "character".

Dundee United began the year 1927 in eighteenth position out of twenty in the First Division with Dundee fifth, but it was United who won the New Year derby match 1-0 with a last-gasp goal from right-back Jock Kay. Both clubs also had a good start in the Cup and a third round tie with Celtic brought a record crowd (37,471) to Dens Park. Unfortunately the match was lost 4-2 and United too went down in the next round 5-0 to Partick Thistle. The Cup was eventually won by Celtic with John Thomson[5] in goal. In the final they defeated Second Division East Fife by three goals.

Cardiff City, however, with Sam Irving in their team, managed to win the FA Cup from the English Second Division and this would serve to give the Fifers continued heart. Alas, more than heart was required to save United who were relegated, along with Morton.

NOTES

1 — "What bloody shits the Dundeans must be," said T E Lawrence (Lawrence of Arabia) on hearing of Churchill's demise. One wonders what he would have thought of that PLO flag in the City Chambers?!

2 — Sam Irving, a Northern Ireland cap.

3 — Jimmy Simpson, father of Ronnie Simpson, later played two great games against Rangers and was transferred to Ibrox in 1927. He enjoyed a successful career there.

4 — Leng himself had begun the process by amalgamating his *Evening Telegraph* with Thomson's *Evening Post* in 1905. The companies were effectively one entity from that date.

5 — Thomson made his debut for Celtic against Dundee at Dens in 1927.

9

THE BIG FOOTBALL event of the late 1920s and early 1930s was the Wembley Wizards' 5-1 thrashing of England in 1928, but the domestic game in Scotland at the time was dominated by a quality Rangers team under Bill Struth, with the main opposition coming from Motherwell, League Champions in 1932 and managed by "Sailor" Hunter, the former Dens Park favourite. A wave of Spiritualism was reported to be passing over Dundee in 1927 but at Dens and Tannadice contact could scarcely be made with the living, such was the moribund state of both clubs. There was actually not a great deal to choose between the two at this time but United would soon learn football's hardest lesson, that inconsistency can sometimes consign a club to a world far removed from that of its traditional rivals.

In spite of relegation, the Tannadice Terrors remained fairly buoyant and found their first "star" player in Duncan Hutchison, a centre-forward and ex-miner[1] from Fife. "Dunky" was just beginning to attract attention when United were drawn at home to Dundee in the second round of the Scottish Cup. He scored two in a match watched by more than 20,000 people. It was not quite enough for although they were twice behind in the game Dundee, augmented by two new English forwards, Whitlow and Lawley, managed a 3-3 draw and won the replay 1-0. But revenge was not long in coming for the next season, and also in the third round of the Cup, the teams met at Dens Park. Hutchison was again the man of the match and although his early goal was equalised by Lawley, United won the replay 1-0. In the fourth round they were unlucky to draw Rangers at Ibrox but performed reasonably well before 50,000 people, going down 3-1.

This disappointment was short-lived, however, for that season (1928-29), United won the Second Division Championship again, and with the following team: McGregor; Taylor and McLure; Dorward, Bain and Deuchar; Ross or Henderson, Hart, Hutchison, Kay and Michie or Cameron. Dundee FC finished third bottom of the First Division and escaped relegation by only three points, but the return of United to the upper bracket gave both clubs a shot in the arm, and local rivalry once again intensified. Before the first derby match could take place (1929), however, the United fans were hit by a bombshell when it was revealed that their hero, Hutchison, for a fee of £4,000 was to team up with the legendary Hugh Gallacher in the colours of United's Newcastle namesakes. The fans were understandably most unhappy about this and when right-winger George Ross was later transferred to Portsmouth, Chairman William Hutchison (no relation) was forced to publicly defend the club's policy. Whilst he recognised the fact that United were one of the best home-supported clubs in the provinces, he said, they would have "gone bust" but for the money received for Hutchison and Ross. Whether or not this was strictly true will never be known but the decisions were taken and the club prepared to accept the consequences.

Both derby matches were won by Dundee that season (1929-30) and the Dark Blues, now under Jimmy Bissett, were beginning to shape up as a good side. The half-back line in particular of McNab, McCarthy and Thomson was very sound and although Thomson was later transferred to Everton, the fans were placated by the return of left-winger Alec Troup back to his old stamping ground. Troup made his return debut in the fourth round Scottish Cup tie against Hearts at Dens and Dundee also signed a promising junior from Violet at this time, although it was in a different shade of blue that Scot Symon would eventually make his name. He came to Dens, however, in the face of stiff competition from other clubs and it was Treasurer William McIntosh who received the credit. Unfortunately such enterprise was not matched across the road and following a disastrous decline at the tail end of the season the Tannadice team were once again relegated.

Season 1930-31 was a better one for both teams. United went straight to the top of the Second Division and by October Dundee were in second position to Celtic in the First. The fact that English clubs had imposed a ban on their Scottish players[2] in respect of playing for their country meant that a number of good home-based Scots got a chance,

Dundee United 1928.
Back Row: W Hutchison, J Brownlie, Dorward, Taylor, McGregor, McLure,
Deuchars, Bain, J Ouskluy (Trainer), E Robertson.
Front Row: B Carnegie, Henderson, Hart, Hutchison, Kay, Michie,
D Walker.

(Courtesy: Dundee Public Library, DC Thomson)

and left-back Jock Gilmour and right-half Colin McNab of Dundee FC both played for Scotland. Indeed, McNab was capped twice against England and in 1931 played his part in a 2·0 victory at Hampden.

Dundee's regular team at this time was Marsh; Brown and Gilmour; McNab, Symon and Blyth; Gavigan, Ritchie, Dempster, Campbell and Troup, and in the second round of the Scottish Cup they beat Rangers 2-1 at Ibrox (Campbell and Robertson scored). Aberdeen, however, were their masters in the next round.[3]

United, meanwhile, scored a record 14-0 victory over Nithsdale Wanderers in the first round of the Cup and in the second round drew Celtic at Tannadice. The first match was postponed but the dream of a Tayside "double" over the Old Firm narrowly failed to come true when United went down 3-2 (Kay and Bennett). The club, however, was holding its position in the League and a 2-1 victory over Dunfermline in the last game of the season at Tannadice was enough to give them promotion (1931).

The thirties was an era of great drama, upheaval and crisis throughout the world. At the beginning of the decade both Gandhi and Al Capone were in the news for breaking the laws of their respective countries, although for different reasons; the great economic depression had led to rioting in cities everywhere including Dundee, where the unemployed who marched against the iniquities of the Means Test[4] were baton-charged by the police and savagely sentenced for retaliation; and a flood-tide of Nationalism[5] began to sweep across the globe, carrying everything with it.

Even in Scottish football there was a tragedy when the unfortunate Sam English of Rangers, having been declared unfit earlier in the week, finally made the team and was involved in a clash with Celtic goalkeeper, John Thomson. Thomson, who had been badly injured before as a result of his bravery, suffered a fractured skull in diving at the forward's feet, and died later that night, 5 September 1931. Some 50,000 people attended his funeral at Cardenden in Fife, but the next day's newspapers suggested that events of a far more dramatic and sinister nature were about to engulf the world. For alongside the photograph of the Thomson mourners was one of a smiling Adolf Hitler. The leader of the German Nazi Party was pleased because the previous day thousands of his followers had openly defied a police ban and worn their brown shirt, paramilitary uniforms at a rally in Gera.

The thirties also witnessed some of the most unusual behind-the-scenes activities in the city of Dundee's footballing history, events which had their origin at the inception of the Dundee United Football Company Ltd.

It will be remembered that the original company directors (May 1925) were William Hogg, a fruit broker; William Hutchison, a wine and spirit merchant; James Dickson, also a publican; Alexander Lamb, a newsagent and tobacconist; David Simpson, a manual teacher, and David Godfrey, a jute merchant (Jimmy Brownlie was Company Secretary). The number of shares sold, however, did not meet the anticipated figure and by October 1925 changes were afoot. First, David Simpson was replaced by David Halley (also a publican) and then a Trust Deed was signed in favour of William Hogg and William Hutchison who, by paying off certain debts at the bank, effectively took control of the club. Hogg and Hutchison then conveyed the assets of the club to themselves as trustees for the debenture holders and when Hogg died in 1927 he was replaced by local builder, John Carnegie who, it was planned, would also receive payment for his work on the ground improvements from gate receipts. He now joined Hutchison and Halley on the United board.

That these men had the interest of Dundee United at heart was not in doubt, but the club was in financial difficulty from the start when its flotation failed to attract support and, as the position deteriorated in the late 1920s, the high ideals of the directors began to slip somewhat. No new stand was built and the gate receipts did not always find their way to the intended sources. This, Hutchison claimed later, was done out of financial necessity as the gate money was required to keep the club alive on a day-to-day basis (hence the Hutchison transfer in 1928) but such methods built up resentment on the board, and matters came to a head following United's promotion in 1931.

By then, Hutchison, Halley and Andrew Boyd Carnegie (son of John, deceased) had a fellow director in Ernest S Robertson (born

Dundee FC 1933.
Back Row: J Brown (Trainer), McCarthy, Morgan, Marsh,
Symon, T Smith, Guthrie.
Front Row: Blyth, Murdoch, Robertson, Mackay, Gilmour, Lee, Paterson,
H Smith.

(Courtesy: DC Thomson)

71

1892). Robertson's father had taken out fifty shares in the Dundee United Football Company in 1926 in the name of his firm, John Robertson and Son, Aerated Water Manufacturers. On 1 December 1928 the company's shares were transferred to Ernest Robertson and on 8 March 1929 he became a director. Season 1930-31 had been a successful playing year culminating in promotion, but the club made a trading loss of £3,112.4s.2d., and its liabilities stood at more than £21,000. At a board meeting on 30 April 1931 Hutchison stepped down as Chairman in favour of E S Robertson, and later Brownlie was replaced as Manager by the ex-Rangers centre-forward, Willie Reid. The managerial job unfortunately proved too much for Reid and United were relegated again in 1932, the third time in five years. Although Hutchison was then replaced as a director the trading position also failed to improve, and for the year ending April 1933 United's auditors, Dickson, McIntyre and Co[6] reported another substantial loss, of £3,327.3s.8d.

At Dens Park there was also trouble in the boardroom and in this case it was William McIntosh who had become disaffected. McIntosh had begun his association with Dundee FC at the turn of the century and was to serve the game in an administrative capacity for more than fifty years. He became treasurer of the club in 1910, a director in 1912, saw through the important structural changes at Dens in the early 1920s and took the club on its first European tours to Spain (1923-24). From 1927-33 he was also treasurer of the SFA and was personally credited with a number of outstanding signings for Dundee FC, including Troup, Cook and Symon. It was indirectly through his other great interest, however — Music Hall — that complications with the club arose.

McIntosh was proprietor of the Opera Bar in Gellatly Street which adjoined His Majesty's Theatre and Opera House (now the site of the ABC cinema) and was well-known in Music Hall circles. When it came to social functions at Dundee Football Club, he was the obvious choice as supplier of refreshments and organiser of entertainment, but after one such occasion the club failed to pay his liquor bill and he sued (successfully) for the sum of £70.1s.3d. Relations with his fellow directors were, therefore, not very good and, sensing a wind of change at Dens (a new board under Wattie Simpson and a new manager, ex-Ranger Billy McCandless, had recently been appointed)[7] he first resigned as treasurer and then began to look elsewhere for a place to deploy his administrative talents. A turn of events at Tannadice soon gave him his opportunity.

United had begun Season 1933-34 calamitously, plunging to the bottom of the Second Division and the debenture holders, their funds exhausted and repayable on 1 January 1935, now sought reconstruction of the company. A committee of debenture holders was appointed to confer with the Directors and Trustees and the prime mover on the committee was one Bailie George Greig, a wholesale tobacconist. The move came too late, for in February 1934, following a Cup exit and a League defeat by bottom club Edinburgh City, the situation was deemed so grave that United offered to resign from the Scottish League. Now "certain parties"[8] it was revealed, had offered their assistance but did not want to disclose their scheme until League sanction was given to the club to withdraw its resignation. At a board meeting on Saturday 24 February 1934 it was approved that these parties would in future control the team, although the Directors would remain in office until the end of the season, when reconstruction would be considered.

The League then accepted a second United letter withdrawing the resignation and this paved the way for what most fans nowadays would regard as the bizarre situation of one man (William McIntosh) becoming a major shareholder of both Dundee United and Dundee FC simultaneously, a state of affairs which was to last for more than twenty years. What made things even more unusual is that McIntosh was one of the Dundee FC officials who opposed the return of Dundee Hibs to the Second Division in 1923, creating a certain amount of animosity between the clubs and their supporters in the process. Football, however, is a funny game, and McIntosh now found himself at Tannadice.

On the playing side Willie Reid "resigned" and the old warhorse Jimmy Brownlie was reinstated as manager with ex-Dundee FC player Sam Irving as his assistant. Brownlie's first signing was also an ex-Dundee FC man, Andrew Campbell, and before the first Saturday match the players were taken for lunch to a local hotel where the first team of the new regime was announced. It was: McIntosh; Willis and Campbell; Corbett, Masson[9] and Lindsay; Ross, Brown, Auchterlonie, Gardner and Laing. Perhaps all they were really needing was a good feed for they thrashed Kings Park 8-1 (with five from Auchterlonie) and the following week beat Leith Athletic 5-2! The crowd (1,500) which turned up for the Kings Park game, however, was quite disappointing and with Lochee Harp pulling 12,622 to a Scotland Junior Cup quarter-final that same month, the new United management obviously had its work cut out.

The new United board — Halley, Carnegie, Robertson, Greig, William Donald (a doctor) and John Millar (a hatter) consituted on 26 September 1935 — was responsible for at least one initiative which was to have far-reaching consequences for the club. The share capital was reduced from £25,000 to £2,500 divided into 25,000 shares of two shillings. The reduction of capital did not involve a diminution of liability and it meant that financial problems would continue to afflict the club, but what it did do was clear the way for a working-class direct-orate which would prove so valuable to United. The company ran into difficulty again in 1936 and George Greig, by lending them more money, became Managing Director with sole control. But even with the support of Robertson he could not get the club back onto a sound financial footing and in 1938, power returned to the "camp" of William Hutchison.

Hutchison, following a Court Case at the First Division of the Court of Session in 1934, had resigned as a Trustee but remained a share-holder, and in 1938 rejoined the board along with Donald, Brownlie, Carnegie and Irving. He later transferred shares to Brownlie and Irving and his directorship went to William McCutcheon (another publican) but with Arthur Cram installed as Company Secretary, the Robertson "faction" once more gained control, and with John Carnegie Jnr adding the shares of the Reilly family to those of his own (Pat Reilly d. 1937) and James Littlejohn replacing Sam Irving, the board took on a degree of stability during the Second World War which it has maintained. William McIntosh was co-opted in 1945 and Ernest Robertson became Chairman in 1948.

NOTES

1 — Dundee FC had their own star players at that time. Inside-left George Gibson and left-winger Willie Cook were later transferred to Bolton Wanderers and formed the left-wing of the Wanderers' side which won the FA Cup in 1929. Cook was also capped.

2 — Scots utterly dominated English football at this time. Jackson, James, Gallacher and Morton were all in their prime and in 1928 Newcastle United fielded a team against Leeds United in which only one player was not Scottish-born.

3 — Again, Jimmy Guthrie's autobiography reveals that Dundee's trainer in the early 1930s was an Evangelist, Jack Brown. His favourite ploy was apparently to set Protestants against Catholics in training but when tensions led to the postponement of a trial match, he was dismissed.

4 — In Dundee in 1932 the number of married women refused benefit was 100 times that of Burnley, an English town of comparable size.

5 — Britain went for a National Government in 1929 when a General Election failed to produce a clear majority for the Labour Party. Against the wishes of many in his party, Ramsay MacDonald went over to the grouping of National Unionists, National Liberals and National Labourites and in 1931 they won a landslide victory in the General Election, greatly reducing Labour's representation and utterly routing Lloyd George's Liberals. Michael Foot's brother, Dingle, was elected as a National Liberal and Frances Horsburgh, a National Unionist (the only Unionist ever to be elected by Dundee) defeating Neddy Scymgeour in the process, but as the thirties progressed, this "National" grouping with first Baldwin then Chamberlain as Prime Minister, became generally seen as a "front" for the Tory party. In Dundee, for example, in 1931 local secondary school teachers were given a pay *cut* of 8%. The National Government then stopped the town's Education Grant of £2,500 which meant that the cut would have to be *increased* to 10%, and school fees at Harris, Morgan and Grove Academies and Lawside Secondary School also increased. Presumably those who could afford to pay the fees (£2-£5 per year) were not on the breadline.

6 — In November 1933 this company took in as a partner the young accountant, James R Gellatly.

7 — Long-standing board members P Jackson, A McBain and W McIntosh were replaced by J W A Simpson, D P How, J Ford and F Graham. Simpson, How and Graham were jute merchants and the first-named reputedly a millionaire.

8 — William McIntosh and George Greig among others.

9 — Bill Masson who also played for Dundee FC and became Director of Physical Education in the town.

10

THE MID-1930s were a boom period for sports-mad Dundonians. As well as being "fitba daft" Dundee was always a great boxing town and the fairground booths threw up some great local fighters like Freddie Tennant, who actually beat the up-and-coming Benny Lynch on two occasions.

Dundee FC opened the 1934-35 season with a victory against Rangers and were congratulated in the official United programme the following week. Both teams were in the top ten of their respective divisions and Dundee FC were getting particularly good service from their new inside-right or right-half Eric (Jimmy) Guthrie. United, meanwhile, signed a promising junior centre-forward called Arthur Milne from Brechin Vics.

In the League, the Dundee teams finished a creditable eighth and fourth in First and Second Divisions, but in the 1935 Scottish Cup, Dundee FC went out 2-1 to Motherwell in the first round. United, however, made a promising start by beating Fraserburgh 6-2 (away) in the first round, and Queen's Park 6-3 (home) in the second (with Milne beating Queen's Park goalie Desmond White four times). George Ross had returned to United (he would later be followed by his old ally Hutchison) and in the third round they drew 2-2 with Hearts at Tynecastle. For the replay at Tannadice, Jimmy Brownlie planned to have an unemployed gate but the idea was vetoed by Hearts and in an incident which again reflects the dire poverty in which some Dundee folk lived, a crowd of around 300 people demonstrated at Tay Bridge station when the Hearts team arrived. The Jammy Tarts won 4-2 after extra time. Rangers eventually won that Cup, and Celtic the League.

In March 1935 Scot Symon asked for a transfer and in the 1935-36 close season he was signed along with Lew Morgan by Portsmouth, a club which was becoming something of a Scots colony at the time. (Guthrie would also join their ranks in 1937). That and the latest local scandal kept the town gossip going. Dundee Labour Councillor John Fraser, following the resignation of Chief Constable John MacDonald, asked the Scottish Secretary of State to initiate an enquiry into the behaviour of Dundee Police Force over the previous five years (MacDonald had lost a £3,000 slander action brought against a Dundee citizen).

The League performances of both clubs were again undistinguished but in the 1936 Cup both did reasonably well. In the first round, Dundee FC beat amateurs Babcock and Wilcox 6-0 at Dens, and United drew 2-2 with Alloa at Tannadice. The United replay was drawn 1-1, and United finally did the business at Tynecastle Park, but the most interesting feature of these games was that the Alloa team contained a fine right-winger called Bill Shankly (whose brother Bob was centre half for Falkirk) and a strong full-back named Jerry Kerr! Both were promising youngsters at the time and both later progressed — Shankly to Carlisle and Preston and Kerr to Rangers, Edinburgh St Bernards and Hibs. In the third round Dundee beat Airdrie 2-1, while United went down 5-3 to Cowdenbeath, but in the fourth round, the Dark Blues crashed out 4-0 to Kilmarnock.

The local game, therefore, was in something of the doldrums but a Scotland-Wales international brightened things up at Dens Park in December 1936 and United fans were once again kept entertained by boardroom machinations at Tannadice. Following a very poor start to season 1936-37 Bailie Greig, who had resigned from the board some time previously, suddenly was called to attend a board meeting. It was later announced that he would assume "complete control". His keen business instinct was thought to have been missed and he immediately sought to get a good price for the in-demand Arthur Milne. "I'm convinced," he was quoted as saying, "Tannadice has immense potentialities — and it's going to my job to capitalise them".

But national issues dominated the news. King Edward VIII was forced to abdicate in favour of his brother George VI as "Morganatic marriage" — to a commoner (and divorcee) — was not possible under British law; 149,407 people (including 50,000 Englishmen) baptised the new Hampden Park; and in the Spanish Civil War German planes (assisting Franco) bombed the Holy Basque city of Guernica, the first air raid on a civilian target. The world had changed, and the game of football had changed in the 1920s and 1930s too, with the offside and penalty rules being upgraded to their current status.

In Dundee it was now Dens Park which was the subject of rumour concerning behind-the-scenes moves and the net result of this was that Billy McCandless "resigned" as manager, to be replaced by another ex-Ranger, Andy Cunningham ("Brainy, breezy and bowler-hatted," said the *Record*, Cunningham was later a noted sports journalist). Arthur Milne meanwhile went on trial with Liverpool but the option was not taken up and he then signed for Hibs, with whom he enjoyed considerable success.[1] Dundee FC finished ninth in the First Division and United fourteenth in the Second.

Season 1937-38 began calamitously for United, who went down 7-1 at home to St Bernards but as so often happens, a change at the top can breathe new life, and Dundee FC started brilliantly, with their team lining up: Marsh; Cowie and Rennie; Laurie, Evans and Smith; Regan, Baxter, Coats, McMenemy and Kirby. (Harry) McMenemy and Regan had been brought north from England at the time Charles Atlas was making his first appearances in the advertising columns offering to convert "YOU!" from a seven-stone weakling to a champion, and Dundee began the season with seven straight victories, establishing a three-point lead at the top of the First Division.

Rangers, of course, were never far behind and the west-coast press was in its usual state of admiration. Pictures, for example, would show "Dougie" Gray of Rangers beating "Warren" of Hearts to the ball. The Light Blues, however, did find a new goalscoring star that season, a young centre-forward called Willie Thornton, while at Parkhead a true goalscoring "great" departed. Jimmy McGrory who had scored 500 goals in fifteen seasons, left to become manager of Kilmarnock.

Sadly, Dundee FC could not keep up their fine form. First, they began to slide from the upper reaches of the League and then they went out of the Cup in the first round, 4-2 to Albion Rovers. United, conversely, had found their form and they provided the big shock in that round of the Cup by defeating Hearts 3-1 at Tannadice, with their team: Nicholson; Collington and Grieve; Skelligan, Watson and Yorke; Duncan Hutchison, Clarkson, Rumbles, Robertson and Adamson. In the second round, however, they had the misfortune to run into the most famous East Fife team of all time, who beat them 5-0 at Methil, then went on to win the Scottish Cup, the first and only Second Division team to do so.

Things were now pretty bleak in Dundee. United were not in the promotion hunt, both teams were out of the Cup, and in spite of a 6-1 victory over Rangers at Dens, Dundee FC had (unbelievably) slipped into the relegation zone of the First Division. On 30 April 1938, their fate was sealed when, with 31 points from 37 games, they drew the final match 0-0 (away) to Ayr United. The same day Queen of the South beat Rangers 3-2 at Ibrox so Dundee FC, a club reputed to have the richest directorate in Scotland[2] at the time, were down along with Morton. No fewer than six clubs finished one point above them, and United fans were equally despondent, for their favourites finished fifth bottom of the Second Division.

By the time the 1938-39 season got under way people were even *more* pessimistic, but now it was the prospect of war which alarmed them. One-quarter of the world was already at war, Hitler, Mussolini and Franco were advancing virtually unchecked by other nations, and photographs of air raid shelters and gas masks began to make their rather ominous appearance in newspapers.

United won the first Second Division derby 3-0 at Tannadice (with English newcomer Horace Wooley scoring twice) two weeks before Neville Chamberlain returned from Munich with his famous "piece of paper" which promised "Peace for our Time"; Rangers signed Scot Symon from Portsmouth who then proceeded to win the 1939 FA Cup with Jimmy Guthrie as captain; and Willie Cook returned to Dens Park and helped Dundee FC first to reverse the earlier derby result and then to attain sixth place in the Second Division (United finished ninth).

By then, however, Madrid had fallen to Franco's Falangists and when it was announced on 21 August 1939 that Stalin had signed a non-aggression pact with the Nazis, people were prepared for the worst. Children were evacuated (in Dundee's case many went to Kincardineshire), Britain re-affirmed its pledge of support to the now-exposed Poland, and when Germany attacked that eternal political whipping-boy on 1 September 1939, Britain and France responded with a declaration of war.

It was hard lines. Dundee FC were top of the Second Division and United second equal.

NOTES

1 — Milne returned to United during wartime. His signing for Hibs cost United money because they had turned down £3,000 from Chelsea in favour of Liverpool's bid. When Liverpool failed to take up their option Milne was not re-transferred to United and Hibs picked him up. United eventually got £750 after a complaint to the League.

2 — J W A Simpson, F Graham, D P How and J A Galloway had made their money in the Indian Jute Trade. The first three acquired their substantial shareholdings in the 1920s when Dundee FC's shares were undersubscribed and money was needed to pay for the re-construction of Dens Park; Galloway came in in 1936 in place of John Ford.

  They gained control of the club in the thirties ousting the "Old Guard" of McIntosh, Jackson and McBain and their methods of management were severely criticised by Jimmy Guthrie who, as a first-team player was faced with proposed wage *cuts* on occasion.

3 — The unlikely name of Sir William Lamond, c/o The Imperial Bank of India, 25 Broad Street, London EC2 also appears on Dundee FC's list of shareholders at this time. His seventy-five shares were later sold to James R Gellatly.

11

DUNDEE FC COMPETED in the East and North East League for one season then went into retirement until 1944. United, however, with Arthur Cram, CA, as club secretary carried on and played throughout the war with the exception of season 1940-41, a move which proved popular among local fans and helped to further consolidate their support. United also competed in the North East League but their real moment of glory was enjoyed in the 1939-40 War Cup.

In the first round played on a home-and-away basis they defeated Partick Thistle 4-2 at Tannadice and drew 1-1 at Firhill; in the second round an Arthur Milne hat-trick was the feature of a 7-1 victory over Third Lanark, Dundee's conquerors in the first round; and in the third, also played at Tannadice, they crushed Kilmarnock 3-0.

Guest players were allowed during wartime and once again the name of Jasper (Jerry) Kerr, now of Hibs, crossed United's path. Kerr played four games at left-back before injury necessitated his replacement by Tommy Dunsmore, also of Hibs, though, in all, only thirteen players were used in the campaign. In the semi-final United met Airdrie and following a 0-0 draw at Easter Road, the Lanarkshire team introduced none other than Stanley Matthews to their side. The great man, however, was played out of the game by Dunsmore and the Terrors marched on to the final with a 3-1 victory.

This final match was played against Rangers at Hampden on 4 May 1940, and the attendance of 71,000 reflected the war-time hunger which existed for the game in Scotland. United lined up: Thomson; Miller and Dunsmore; Baxter, Littlejohn and Robertson; Glen, Gardner, Milne, Adamson and Fraser, and since the club was manager-less (an ex-Morton and Rangers player, Robert McKay,[1] had come and gone with the onset of war) a Lochee businessman named Jimmy Allan helped look after the team.[2] Inside-left Adamson had the ball in the net in the first half but the "score" was disallowed and an inevitable late goal from Rangers' Smith sent the Tannadice men home empty-handed. It had been a great effort, though.

After the war the ubiquitous William MacIntosh and James Littlejohn, the war-time centre-half, joined Ernest Robertson, J Carnegie, Arthur Cram and Chairman W McCutcheon on the United board and the appointment of Mr Littlejohn was particularly significant as it reinforced United's policy of having ex-top-class players not only in the manager's chair but actually *on the board*. Jimmy Brownlie and Sam Irving, for example, were pre-war directors, Duncan Hutcheson would later follow suit and eventually become chairman of the board, and Littlejohn's association has carried on into the 1980s.

Dundee FC by comparison still tended to go for directors who were *primarily* substantial local businessmen and one cannot but reflect that such a policy, inasmuch as it has continued, has not had a wholly beneficial effect upon the club in the longer term. In the immediate post-war period, however, it was the Dundee FC board which got its equation right and it was a former player who proved to be the crucial factor.

It is difficult to overestimate the contribution George Anderson made to Dundee Football Club, but if any one man can be said to have consolidated their position as a leading provincial club and to have firmly established their reputation as, traditionally, a good footballing side, then Anderson was the man. An Aberdonian by birth, he had played in goal for Aberdeen FC and later served as a director at that club, but he also turned out for Dundee FC during the First World War and it was in their temporary demise that he saw his opportunity. In 1944 he built a new board around himself and together they faced the "new" world.

In 1943 the war-hero Churchill had been offered the freedom of Dundee, which he declined, but in 1945 it was once again his turn to be rejected, this time by the people of Britain in a General Election. The city elected two political inside-lefts — John Strachey and Tom Cook — in a Labour landslide and now prepared for a period of reconstruction and relative prosperity as new and more diversified industry was

Dundee United FC War Cup Finalists 1940.
Left to Right: Littlejohn, Kerr, Thomson, Pinkerton, Miller, Brand,
Robertson, Dunsmore, Baxter, Fraser, Milne, Hutton, Adamson, Glen,
Gardiner.

(Courtesy: DC Thomson)

Adamson "scores" against Rangers in the War Cup Final. The "goal" was
disallowed.

(Courtesy: DC Thomson)

brought to the town.

United also had a new manager in Willie McFadyen, the ex-Motherwell star, but it was Anderson — "Toffee Dod"[3] as the players called him — who continuously made the running. Right from the start he showed himself to be a progressive football thinker, emphasising ballwork in training and psychology in man-management and public relations, and in the early fifties he actually called for a smaller, premier-style Super League on a number of occasions. Of course, it is often said that football is about players but in this department Anderson also had a good eye. Doug Cowie, a young half-back from Aberdeen St Clements, was picked up in the face of stiff competition; Tommy Gallacher (son of Patsy), who had guested during the war, joined the club on a permanent basis from Queen's Park; Reg Smith, a skilful Englishman, who had also guested, came from Millwall; and no less an authority than Matt Busby commented publicly on the club's cultured syle of play. Both Dundee and Dundee United were in the Scottish League "B" Division in season 1945-46, but at the turn of the year Dundee were top and United bottom and in the January Derby, Dundee won 3-2 at Tannadice (recently stepped with railway sleepers).

Dundee FC actually topped the North East League in 1944-45 and the "B" Division in 1945-46, but it was not until the conclusion of their third season of "supremacy" that League reconstruction allowed them to progress to the "A" Division. By this time another war-time guest made-permanent, Sammy Cox, had gone to Rangers to be replaced by Alf Boyd from St Johnstone, and a strong unorthodox centre-forward, Albert Juliussen, had written his unusual name in the history books. At two consecutive games in March 1947 Juliussen scored double hat-tricks, the first at Alloa in a 10-0 victory and the second (seven goals actually) against Dunfermline at Dens, where the same score was registered. The double figures in successive games was also a record and Dundee FC were definitely now giving notice that as a club they were coming on-stream. Rangers won the "A" Division that season (1946-47); Aberdeen (managed by Davie Halliday) took the Scottish Cup for the first time; and two new stars appeared in a Scottish jersey — inside-forward Billy Steel of Morton and Gordon Smith of Hibs, a right-winger who had been signed from Dundee North End.

At the beginning of 1948, Dundee lay fourth in a First Division of sixteen teams and United twelfth out of sixteen in the Second

Dundee FC League Cup Winners 1951.
Back Row: Cowan, Gallacher, Brown, Toner, Cowie, Christie, Follon.
Front Row: Pattillo, Boyd, George Anderson (Manager), Steel, Flavell.

(Courtesy. DC Thomson)

Division, but United still had ambitions which were regularly aired in public and it should also be remembered that a number of clubs with a distinguished history (e.g. St Bernards) had failed to survive the wartime break. United also maintained their reputation for finding new talent, and forwards in particular. Outside-left George "Piper" MacKay was swapped for Dundee centre-half Jim Dickson and, ironically, it was Dickson who did particularly well in the Tannadice defence, although they did lose five goals to Birmingham City in a friendly (the Birmingham players and officials were later presented with Timex watches, one of the new local products of which Dundonians were understandably proud). MacKay was followed into the United forward-line meanwhile by his namesake, centre-forward Peter MacKay, but even his considerable goalscoring talents[4] could not raise the club from its lowly position. Rangers were also struggling to find form in the "A" Division and the *Courier* managed to get in on the "What's wrong at Ibrox?" act. Whatever was wrong at Ibrox, the 1947-48

League went to Hugh Shaw's brilliant Hibs side — the first time a provincial club had taken the title since Motherwell in 1932 — and this victory heralded the greatest years in the Edinburgh club's history, "Famous Five" Smith, Johnstone, Reilly, Turnbull, Ormond, *et al.*

Dundee FC were also entering their most consistent period to date and the fourth position in the 1947-48 League was a foretaste of things to come. Again Anderson's foresight was in evidence for, following public statements that star players were not for sale and that young talent would be encouraged, the club proceeded to do just that. Out of the thirty-two players on the books at the beginning of season 1948-49, twenty had come from juvenile or junior ranks and from eight who had come from local clubs, six were in the first team which went into the New Year in third top place.

The Dens Parkers were therefore attracting all the attention on Tayside, but things suddenly changed on 22 January 1949, when United played Celtic at Tannadice in the first round of the Scottish Cup. The game attracted 25,000 people and afterwards was described as "the greatest cup tie ever seen in Dundee". United tackled the Celts with great enthusiasm and in all had the ball in the Bhoys' net seven times, although only four counted. United took the lead, then went two ahead before Celtic pulled them back. United then went ahead again, and again the Celts equalised before the Terrors grabbed the winner. I think it was around this time that the saying "Dens Park for skills, Tannadice for thrills" originated and the United heroes on this occasion were: Edmiston; Berrie and Jardine; Ogilvie, Ross and Grant; Quinn, Dickson, MacKay, Mitchell and Cruickshank. Right-winger Frank Quinn, himself an ex-Celt, was one of the big stars of the United side and the scorers were Peter MacKay (2), Dickson and Cruickshank.[5] Unfortunately, the next round saw them in considerably less devastating form and the team lost 3-1 at Tannadice following a 1-1 away draw with Dumbarton.

Dundee FC meanwhile had the First Division's leading goalscorer in centre-forward Alec Stott; lay in second place to the Hibs in "A" Division; and progressed to the semi-final of the Cup where they lost 2-1 to Clyde. By the time that game had taken place, however, they had secured a 4-3 victory over the Hibs and sat on top of the League until the last game which they had to win at Falkirk to become champions for the first time. Dundee's team was: Lynch; Follon and Irvine; Gallacher, Cowie and Boyd; Gunn, Patillo, Stott, Gerrie and Hill. In the first half Stott missed a penalty when Hill was brought down, and the Falkirk goalkeeper followed this up with a wonder save from Gerrie. It was not to be the Dark Blues' day obviously and in the second half Falkirk scored four times with one reply from Dundee. Tommy Gallacher later blamed the defeat on an uncharacteristic error of judgement by George Anderson, who locked himself and the team in the dressing room for an hour before the kick-off, thus unnerving the players. The team had not yet peaked, however, and with James Gellatly installed as chairman and Anderson as Managing Director, they looked likely to come again.

In 1949 Anderson signed a brilliant young goalkeeper from Carnoustie Panmure, the lanky Bill Brown, and he made his debut for the reserve team on 10 October against Raith Rovers. A Canadian, Jack Cowan, and two South Africans, Gordon Frew and Ken Ziesing, were then fixed up and on 21 September 1950, Anderson pulled off what was generally hailed as the transfer coup of the century when he paid Derby County £17,500 for one of Scotland's greatest-ever inside-

Dundee United FC 1949.
Back Row: Hart (Trainer), Berrie, Jardine, Edmiston, Ogilvie, Ross, Dewar, Grant.
Front Row: Quinn, Dickson, Mckay, Mitchell, Smart.

(Courtesy: DC Thomson)

87

forwards, Billy Steel.

Steel's transfer was indeed a bold move, but also a wise one in that whereas Dundee's defence was settled, the attack was not, and Steel provided the craft to bring out the best in the front line. His own career was fairly turbulent, ending in dispute both at Derby and Dens, and he was the first Scotland player to be ordered off, but his talent was undeniable and his debut for Dundee on 23 September was watched by 34,000 people. Also, with admission prices ranging from 1s 6d for the ground to 5s for the centre stand, he chalked £4,000 off his transfer fee straight away and, as the *Courier* reported, all this fitted nicely into Anderson's "master plan". In the game, Dundee beat Aberdeen 1-0 and by New Year 1951 they topped the First Division with United in second place in the Second Division. Arguments about the respective merits of the two teams were also (temporarily) settled later that month when they were drawn against each other in the Scottish Cup and United fans must have thought they had it in the bag when they got a 1-1 draw at Dens. In an otherwise fine game, however, the United goalkeeper Wylie blundered once and Dundee FC scraped a 1-0 victory in the replay. Raith Rovers finally put Dundee FC out in the fourth round but both Dundee and United maintained their league challenge and finished third and fourth in their respective Divisions.

At Dens Park though, not everyone was pleased with the way things were going and in April 1951, ex-Bailie John Thomson, a former chairman of the club, resigned from the board of directors in protest at what he saw as George Anderson having too much of a free hand. But Anderson's policies were to be vindicated the following season.

In the League Cup Section C, Dundee faced stiff opposition from Hearts, Raith Rovers and St Mirren, but they qualified with a last-gasp victory at Starks Park. In the quarter-final they faced Falkirk, now in the Second Division, but the only unbeaten side in the country, and the Taysiders got through by drawing 0-0 at Brockville and winning 2-1 at Dens. In the semi-final Celtic and Rangers, who so often seemed to avoid each other on such occasions, were paired together (the game was won by Rangers) and Dundee booked their ticket to Hampden with a 5-1 victory over Motherwell.

On 22 October 1951, Dundee FC faced Rangers with the following side: Brown; Follon and Cowan; Gallacher, Cowie and Boyd; Toner, Patillo, Flavell,[6] Steel and Christie. Rangers scored first through Findlay, but any thoughts that this might finish it were dispelled when Flavell equalised early in the second half. In the 69th minute thirty-seven-year-old Johnny (Straight-Back) Patillo put Dundee ahead with another fine shot, but Rangers equalised when a George Young free-kick could only be parried into the net by Brown. The Dundee players claimed that the goalkeeper had been fouled by Willie Thornton, but to no avail, and the match went into extra time. With less than a minute to go Dundee got a free-kick at the corner of the box on the South Stand side. Steel — who was later described as the real architect of the victory — floated it to the far post and there was skipper Alfie Boyd to head the ball into the net. Six thousand Dundee fans savoured their first real moment of glory for more than forty years. (Att. 92,325).

George Anderson praised the coaching of Reggie Smith and the training of Reuben Bennet, and he described the result as a dream come true. Once again the train was met by thousands of fans at the station — by a strange coincidence the Dundee West railway policeman, James Goldie of Lochee, had also officiated forty-one years earlier when the Scottish Cup came home — and the players struggled to Yeaman Shore where a bus took them for a triumphant drive through the town centre and then on to Chairman Gellatly's house for a champagne party.

This was a good time for the city. Morgan Academy pupils won Radio Top of the Form (television was now also on the way); Frankie Quinn was selected for Scotland's "B" team; and that same season (1951-52) Dundee reached the Scottish Cup Final — although Motherwell's tactics of blotting out Steel paid off, and they handed out a 4-0 defeat. In this game Bobby Henderson replaced Brown in goal (debarred by RAF duties) and George "Pud" Hill was on the right-wing in place of Jimmy Toner, but disappointment soon turned to joy when the following season the club went once again to the final of the League Cup, where they met "B" Division Kilmarnock who had defeated Rangers in the semi. Dundee FC's team was: R Henderson; Follon, Frew; Ziesing, Boyd and Cowie; Toner, A Henderson,[7] Flavell, Steel and Christie.

Manager George Anderson was taken ill before the game and a commentary was relayed to him at an Aberdeen nursing home. Reg Smith was a capable deputy, however, and two goals in the last ten minutes from Flavell gave Dundee a hard-fought victory (Att. 51,830). Dundee FC were the first club to win the League Cup in successive years and if anyone had thought up the term "New Firm" in those days, then they and Hibs would have been the obvious candidates.

NOTES

1 — McKay only lasted for two months but in that time it was he who fixed up Jerry Kerr.

2 — Ex-Dundee FC player later assisted Cram in the United camp.

3 — R S McColl, founder of the High Street sweetshop chain, played for Queen's Park at the turn of the century and had the nickname "Toffee Bob". Anderson's name was a corruption of this as he was also in the confectionary business.

4 — Emilio Pacione was a regular goalscorer for United. He scored thirty-three goals between 1945 and 1950. Frank Quinn scored ninety times between 1948 and 1954. Peter MacKay scored 238 in 202 games over roughly the same period.

5 — Dundee also had a notable first round victory over Celtic, 2-1 at Dens, in Season 1946-47.

6 — Bobby Flavell who had come from Hearts had also played in South America with Bogata, where one of his team-mates was Alfredo di Stefano.

7 — Albert Henderson who had a long playing career with Dundee and St Mirren and went on to manage Arbroath.

12

IF THE 1920s AND 1930s were times of political revolution, then the 1950s and 1960s will be remembered for their social revolution, the "Revolt into Style", as George Melly has described the period. In 1953, however, international relations stood deadlocked in the "Cold War" and neither America's new President, Eisenhower, nor Stalin's successors, Malenkov and Bulganin, looked as though they were going to do very much to alter that state of affairs.

Dundee East had a new Labour MP in George Thomson; Cowie and Steel played for Scotland at Wembley in a 2-2 draw; and Bobby Ancell became manager of Dunfermline, with Andy Dickson as trainer. Billy Steel unfortunately was beginning to lose the place at Dens and his departure to the United States would not be long delayed. Elsewhere two ex-Dundee juniors, Jackie Mudie and Ewen Fenton, played their part in Blackpool's "Matthews Cup Final" victory; Mount Everest was climbed for the first time; and Elizabeth II became Queen.

United went out of the Scottish Cup in the first round to Berwick Rangers, losing 3-2 at Tannadice, Dens Park had its biggest-ever crowd[1] and in May 1953 Dundee toured South Africa where they were greeted by some 5,000 people at the airport. This tour helped establish a link between the city's footballing fraternity and that country which has existed until this day, and two right-backs in particular, would benefit from the long trek. A third, Gerry Follon, was involved in an interesting local dispute. Follon was a schoolteacher in Dundee and after some debate was barred from the South African Tour by the local authority — not on moral grounds as might be the case nowadays — but because teachers were in short supply.

91

In 1954 United suffered a record 12-1 defeat at the hands of Mother-well and Dundee FC faced a similar humiliation soon afterwards when they lost 3-0 to "C" Division Berwick Rangers in the third round of the Cup. Duncan Hutchison was re-elected to the United board (he had first been co-opted as a director the previous year); Scot Symon became manager of Rangers in succession to Bill Struth; and another ex-Ranger, Willie Thornton, was invited to take over as manager at Dens (Anderson had resigned through ill health). At Tannadice, Peter MacKay's goalscoring feats had attracted the attention of the local Burnley scout, Jimmy Scott, and he was transferred to that club, but United had a ready-made replacement in the burly, young Fifer Johnny Coyle, and when Reg Smith was appointed manager in succession to McFadyen, United's prospects looked somewhat brighter. Smith, I imagine, would have been rather disappointed at being overlooked for the Dundee job and so not for the first (nor the last) time, a "Dundee" man took the short walk down Tannadice Street.

Scottish football in the early 1950s was a mixture of full-time and part-time players, but players, managers and coaches were beginning to adopt a more professional attitude and the necessity of such an approach was underlined when Hungary — the "Magical Magyars", including the brilliant forwards Sandor, Kocsis, Hidegkuti, Puskas and Fenyvesi — visited Hampden. The advice of *Sporting Post* columnist "Rambler" to the Scotland team was to "come out fighting" but like everyone else who played the game more or less fairly, Scotland were taken apart by the Hungarians. The following week "Rambler", obviously in a state of shock, gibbered, "I think we have a good way to go before we reach the end of the road towards the top again"!

Two significant additions were made to the United board in 1955 in Johnstone Grant, a haulage contractor, and George Fox, a Chartered Accountant, but both United and Dundee were languishing in mid-table positions and United were later said to be £10,000 in debt at this time. Both clubs continued to enjoy good individual performances from the likes of Coyle who was now one of the most consistent goalscorers in the "B" Division and Cowie, one of the most polished midfield players in Division "A" and who attracted a bid from Cardiff City. Cowie was reluctant to move for domestic reasons, however, and Cardiff switched their attentions to his clubmate, centre-half Danny Malloy, who duly signed, for £17,500.

Hibs at their first attempt reached the semi-final of the new European Cup (1956)[2] and in the League Cup that year Dundee FC and United were drawn against each other in the quarter-finals, played home and away. Dundee players were: Brown; Reid and Irvine; Henderson, McKenzie, and Cowie; Chalmers, Black, Merchant, O'Hara and Christie. United were represented by: Edmiston; Young and Briggs; Will, Cross and Stewart; Sturrock, Aikman, John Coyle, Reid and (Maurice) Milne.

Dundee FC as the full-timers were seen to be much fitter in the first leg, which they won by seven goals to three, with Jim Chalmers scoring four, but in the second leg United, strengthened by new signing right-back Davie Gray, showed that they were always a difficult team to beat at Tannadice and won 2-1. An anonymous fan was quoted in the *Record* as saying that had United gone into the first game with more concentration they would have reached the semis, thereby underlining the conventional United wisdom, that they were always as good a side as Dundee. In the semi final, the game against Partick Thistle was drawn 0-0 with seventeen-year-old Alan Cousin coming into conten-

William McIntosh (in foreground) c. 1952.
McIntosh served both Dundee United and Dundee FC in a long administrative career. He was SFA Treasurer and had been at Dens Park for more than twenty years when a boardroom "coup" forced him out in 1933. He then "crossed the road" and served United for another twenty years. Duncan Hutchison is fourth from the left.

(Courtesy: DC Thomson)

tion for a place for the first time, but the replay, under the Ibrox lights, was lost 3-2.

Hugh Robertson, a left-winger from Auchinleck Talbot was the next young hopeful to sign for Dundee, and Bobby Cox the next to make the first team. Rock 'n roll had arrived (although it would be another two years before Tommy Steele was quite badly injured by ecstatic fans following a concert in the Caird Hall), but while it was evidently great to be young, the local headlines belonged neither to pop stars nor footballers. Instead they concentrated on a twenty-year-old Dundee boxer named Dick McTaggart.

McTaggart, an apprentice butcher and one of six boxing brothers, had slowly been picking up a reputation as an amateur lightweight. As ABA champion he was one of five unanimous choices for the British Olympic team (Melbourne, December 1956) and not only did he win the Gold Medal at his weight, but also the prestigious Val Barker Trophy as the most stylish boxer at the Games. Two thousand Dundonians made his return triumphal and he also showed the trophy at Dundee FC's next home game.

Johnny Coyle carried on in season 1956-57 where he had left off the previous year and once again he was the Second Division's second top scorer, but any possible moves were suspended when Reg Smith was suddenly offered the Falkirk job in succession to Bob Shankly who had left Brockville after 23 years as player and manager. This was a disappointment for the United fans as the former English cap had embarked upon a long-term plan for the club and to a certain extent the feeling was mutual, for before he left Smith paid tribute to the United board for trying to hold on to their players. Falkirk, however, were a "bigger" club than United at the time and so the move represented an opportunity to try out some of his more progressive ideas, ideas which bore fruit almost immediately, for in his very first Scottish Cup campaign as manager (1957) he actually brought the cup to Brockville, beating Kilmarnock 2-1 in extra-time of the final replay! The Falkirk team contained the brother of a Dundee FC player (Eddie O'Hara); the two men who had just left Dundee FC (George Merchant and Andy Irvine); a man who would subsequently play for Dundee FC (Bert Slater); and one who would do likewise for United (Doug Moran, scorer of the winning goal). Add Bob Shankly and Reg Smith to that list and it makes most interesting reading. Shankly now moved to Third Lanark.

Dundee's "secret weapon" for the South African tour of 1953. Manager
George Anderson told the press of a "secret weapon", in order to gain
publicity (and crowds) – George "Pud" Hill spills the beans.

(Courtesy: George Hill, DC Thomson)

No managerial appointment was made immediately at Tannadice,
thus leaving Ally Gallacher (Assistant Manager) and Archie Coats
(trainer, ex-Dundee) in charge of the team, but later that year (1957)
the job was filled by Tommy Gray, the former Dundee player and
Arbroath manager, and one of his early duties was to transfer Coyle to
Clyde, for £8,000. Johnny had scored 45 goals, 41 goals and 20 goals to
date in three seasons and he, too, proved to be the missing link at *his*
new club which, remarkably, won the 1958 Scottish Cup with Coyle
scoring the winning goal in the final against Hibs. Sometime, one
could not help but think, some of this outgoing luck was bound to make
the return journey . . .

Hearts, with Dave Mackay as captain, won the First Division
Championship; Elvis Presley was drafted; and the Busby Babes — the
brilliant young Manchester United team — were decimated by an air

crash at Munich. Busby himself had just accepted the job as Scotland team manager and his club side which had reached the semi-final of the European Cup would possibly have been the first British team to win that trophy. Football went into a state of shock. It came back to life however, in the summer of 1958 when the phenomenal seventeen-year-old Brazilian, Pele, appeared in the World Cup Finals in Sweden and performed at the very highest level.

Dundee United also discovered a fine young player that season (1957-58) in Ronnie Yeats, a centre-half and giant of an Aberdonian around whom a new team would be built, though it would take another two years and two changes of management. Similar changes were afoot at Dunfermline FC whom Bobby Ancell left for Motherwell to be succeeded by Andy Dickson, and in Los Angeles a young starlet named Joan Collins was quoted as saying that she never allowed her "dates" to say their "Goodnights" in her Hollywood flat, but took her leave of them on the doorstep. Oh, really?

Season 1958-59 began promisingly for both clubs and when Dundee FC won 2-0 at Ibrox the *Daily Record* said, "Dundee have the makings of a team that could win the Scottish Cup..." By now Alan Cousin was a Scottish League "cap"; a fine young player from Westrigg Bluebell, Alex Hamilton, had taken over "Shug" Reid's right-back position; and an outstanding prospect named Jimmy Gabriel was at centre-half. Dundee FC then picked up a top-class young Fifer, fifteen-year-old Andy Penman, a Scottish Schoolboy cap who had been unhappy with his first choice, Everton. All in all, things actually did seem to be quite healthy at Dens — when disaster struck.

In the first round of the Scottish Cup (31 January 1959) Dundee FC were drawn away to Fraserburgh, a Highland League club consisting of the usual mix of tradesmen, students and others. Dundee lined up: Brown; Hamilton and Cox; Henderson, Gabriel and Cowie; Curlett, Bonthrone, Cousin, Sneddon and Robertson; and the *Record* confidently backed its earlier judgement, predicting that Dundee would "saunter to success". In fact, they sauntered to failure for in a nightmare match they lost a goal in 46 minutes which proved to be decisive.

Emergency bells were now ringing at Dens Park and it was expected they would be forced into the transfer market. Davie Sneddon, signed from Kilwinning Rangers in 1954, went to Preston for £12,000 in April 1959 and two months later Bill Brown, arguably Scotland's

Johnny Coyle (Dundee United).

(Courtesy: DC Thomson)

finest-ever goalkeeper followed Dave Mackay to Tottenham Hotspur for £17,500.

United were not involved in much high finance, but they too were in trouble in that they had slumped to third bottom place in the Second Division.

NOTES

1 — 43,024 people watched Dundee *v* Rangers in February 1953.

2 — Aberdeen actually won the 1954-55 League, but entry to the first Champions' Cup was by invitation.

3 — Manchester United were beaten 5-1 at Dens in a friendly in 1956. Their team contained a number of star players and a young Bobby Charlton, whose debut it was for the club.

97

13

THE YEAR 1959 marks the beginning of what might be called the "modern era" in Dundee football and just as managerial changes precipitated new eras in the 1920s and 1940s, so it was in the 1960s.

Although Manager Willie Thornton left Dundee FC for Partick Thistle in September 1959 he did so for domestic reasons and acknowledged that he was leaving a healthier club both in footballing and financial terms than he was joining. With the transfer of Bill Brown, Dundee FC were in a sound financial position and they used the money to install floodlights and build the covered enclosure opposite the main stand. United were at something of a low ebb in their football but they too were reasonably healthy financially now, thanks mainly to the success of their Taypools operation which had begun in 1956 and which would also provide the money to pay for ground improvements. The ex-Dundee full-back and trainer, Andy McCall, had taken over from Tommy Gray as manager at Tannadice, but was singularly unsuccessful and on 6 July 1959, United made a new managerial appointment which was to have far-reaching consequences.

Jerry Kerr had captained the club during their successful wartime Cup run and when his playing career was over he managed first, Berwick Rangers and then Alloa, where he signed two brilliant inside-forwards who proceeded to hand out regular footballing lessons to other Second Division clubs, United included. One was the legendary John White who would soon leave Falkirk for Spurs before being tragically killed by lightning, and the other Denis Gillespie who was one of Kerr's earliest signings and one of the most significant. On 16 April 1958 Alloa, managed by Kerr, had beaten United 7-1 at

Dundee United 1960.
Back Row: A Coates (Trainer), Graham, MacFadyen, Brown, Neilson, Yeats,
Fraser, Briggs, J Kerr (Manager).
Front Row: Norris, Irvine, Campbell, Gillespie, Ormond.

(Courtesy: DC Thomson)

Tannadice, with White scoring five and Gillespie two. Jerry Kerr's one promise to the United board on taking up the appointment was that he would improve their (third bottom) League position.

At Dens the manager's job went to the now-successful Third Lanark boss, Bob Shankly who, it was reported, had earlier turned down the United job, and he inherited a number of fine players including Pat Liney, Alex Hamilton, Bobby Cox, Ian Ure, Andy Penman, Alan Cousin, Alan Gilzean and Hugh Robertson — although some of them still had to establish themselves in the first team.

Season 1959-60, however, belonged to United. Happy with his goal-keeper, Alec Brown, centre-half Ronnie Yeats and right-winger Bobby Norris, Kerr at once set about strengthening his team in other positions. Apart from Gillespie, right-half Peter Smith came from Hearts, inside-right Jim Irvine and right-half Tommy Graham from junior

99

football, left-half Stewart Fraser from the Army, and if Yeats was unavailable because of *his* Army duties, he had a capable deputy in another young Aberdonian, Doug Smith, although Kerr did sign a third centre-half, David Kidd, from Alloa. Right-half Tommy Neilson was then signed from East Fife and he was joined by another wing-half or inside-forward Dave Whytock[1] from Brechin City. With Eric Walker then coming from Alloa and Gibby Ormond (brother of Willie) from Airdrie, Kerr's side was almost complete and at the turn of the year United, in second place, and their League leaders, St Johnstone, drew 1-1 at Perth before 16,000 people. This was obviously going to be the club's strongest promotion challenge since 1930-31.

Yeats, in particular, was proving to be a tower of strength, and with the arrival of RAF man Jimmy Briggs at left-back the defence became more or less settled. Recognising the need for a final push, however, Kerr then pulled out an ace in Albion Rovers' top-scoring centre-forward Tommy Campbell. His specialist touch enabled the Terrors to sustain their challenge.

Things were also looking up in the local newspaper for Tommy Gallacher, the ex-Dundee half-back, now became football correspondent for the *Courier*, and coverage improved dramatically in its style and content, and in spite of (continuing) complaints of a Dundee FC bias in the paper, it was Gallacher who first promoted United to a regular "top spot" in the sports page if he thought their game merited it. In one match, for example, United had an important 3-1 victory over Montrose at Links Park and this "counter attraction" said the *Courier*, kept the attendance at Dens Park down to 7,000. United were on their way.

On the same day, Jerry Kerr departed from a personal rule by signing an outside-right named Walter Carlyle from Shettleston Juniors without having seen him play. He was in for a surprise! Besides being a good player, the fair-haired Carlyle turned out to be a tremendous character and crowd-pleaser who became famous for goals from "impossible" angles and other "eccentric" play.

Dundee FC, meanwhile, transferred nineteen-year-old Jimmy Gabriel to Everton for an incredible £30,000 and his replacement was another striking, blond-haired half-back from Ayr, Ian Ure; Everton's neighbours Liverpool, now managed by Shankly's brother, Bill, hanselled the Dundee FC floodlights (Dundee won 1-0); and Yeats, Campbell and Ormond got a game for the Second Division Select against

100

Tannadice Park, January 1961.

(Courtesy: DC Thomson)

the Under-23s. Such was Yeats' importance to United, he would occasionally be flown to games from Aldershot or even Germany, but Kerr's judgement was sound for, with Queen of the South and Hamilton stumbling in the run-up, United reached the last game needing to beat Berwick Rangers at Tannadice to join champions St Johnstone in the First Division. They lined up: Brown; Graham and McFadyen (Briggs was injured); Neilson, Yeats and Fraser; Norris, Irvine, Campbell, Gillespie and Ormond. Sixteen thousand people attended the match and the team was on £500 "talent money" to be shared among them if they won, which they duly did, by one goal to nil, Tommy Campbell scoring in the ninth minute.[2]

NOTES

1 — Whytock failed to gain a regular place in the first team but had a successful academic career and was the prospective Labour candidate for Dundee East when he was killed in a car crash prior to the 1979 General Election.

2 — Andy Dickson became physiotherapist at Tannadice and Sammy Kean trainer at Dens Park.

14

THE SUMMER OF 1960 saw Dick McTaggart collect another Olympic medal, this time a bronze in Rome; Scotland hosted one of the best football games of all time when Real Madrid defeated Eintracht Frankfurt 7-3 in the European Cup Final at Hampden; and United's man-of-the-moment Jerry Kerr kept up his astonishing workrate by visiting the Frankfurt club after the final to try to learn something of their methods. He also signed an Italian-born goalkeeper, Roland Ugolini, from Wrexham and promoted both he and Walter Carlyle to the first team; and the club won its first match 2-1 away to Stirling Albion.

At Dens Park, Bob Shankly signed a cultured right-half, Bobby Seith, from English champions Burnley; chose Pat Liney as the successor to Bill Brown (one of Liney's rivals had been the curiously-named Charlie Pllu); and watched Alan Gilzean embark upon his goalscoring odyssey for the club. Dundee FC looked on paper to be the stronger of the city teams, but it was United who won the first derby match, 3-1 at Tannadice, and they then briefly topped the First Division on goal average. Reg Smith, now the manager of Millwall, was said to be interested in a young Hamilton Accies right-winger, Jim McLean (he eventually went to Clyde); Ian McColl, astonishingly, was asked to become Scotland team manager whilst still a Rangers player; and John Fitzgerald Kennedy became the first Roman Catholic President of the United States. He wouldn't have got a game for Rangers, though, as the Ibrox club continued to pursue an anti-Catholic policy.

Neilly Mochan signed for United from Celtic, although he was

Dundee FC Scottish League Champions 1961/62.
Back Row: Smith, Penman, Seith, Stuart, Liney, Wishart, Brown, Waddell,
L Smith (Physio), Gilzean, Ure.
Front Row: S Kean (Trainer), Hamilton, J Swadel (Director), Cox,
J A Gellatly (Chairman), Cousin, R Crichton (Director), Robertson,
R Shankly (Manager).

(Courtesy: DC Thomson)

approaching the veteran stage; Bobby Wishart was brought to Dens Park from Aberdeen; and Dundee FC played Valenciennes in the new Friendship Cup. Jimmy Hill, the ex-Fulham player, was making waves as Chairman of the English Players' Union and a new deal was on the way for footballers in both England and Scotland. Tannadice began its long-awaited facelift with an L-shaped stand and floodlights; and Dundee itself saw some dramatic changes as the old heart was torn out of the city to make way for the new Overgate development.

At Dens an era ended when Bob Shankly announced the departure of that great servant, Doug Cowie, the last of George Anderson's signings, and in doing so, Shankly gave notice that he had definite plans for what *his* team would be and how it would play. The short-ball game at which Cowie excelled would give way to a new-style geared towards the strong front-runners Cousin and Gilzean. Cowie had

103

given 446 performances in 15 years and earned himself 23 caps. He now moved to Morton as player/coach.[1]

Yuri Gagarin of Russia was the first man in space; Frank Haffey of Celtic was almost the first goalkeeper in space when he lost nine playing for Scotland at Wembley; and the astutely-managed Tottenham Hotspur won the English Cup and League "double", the first team to do so since Aston Villa in 1897.

United also finished one point ahead of Dundee FC at the end of their first season in the First Division for forty years, but it was the Dark Blues who had the more settled team and when Gordon Smith, the "Stanley Matthews" of Scottish Football, signed for them on a free transfer from Hearts in June 1961, Shankly's jig-saw was complete. Neither Dundee FC nor United qualified from their League Cup section, however, and United's balance sheet showed a loss of £13,754, so a transfer was on the cards and the obvious candidate was the brilliant Yeats. He eventually moved to Liverpool and is generally recognised as the first rock upon which Bill Shankly built that great modern club. The fee was £30,000. Ure, Gilzean, Penman and Gillespie got Scottish League Caps — in Gillespie's case it was a first for United and he was also named in Scotland's World Cup pool along with Hamilton, Seith, Ure, Gilzean and Robertson. Indeed, of the Dundee FC side, only Pat Liney remained uncapped and this was reflected in the club's League position as they raced to the top of the table, at one stage going 19 games without defeat.

Inevitably Rangers were not far away and with games in hand, so the match at Ibrox on 11 November 1961 was eagerly anticipated. On that foggy afternoon Dundee Football Club demonstrated their championship potential by recording one of the greatest victories in their history. Alan Gilzean scored four, and Andy Penman one, in a 5-1 away triumph, and membership of their supporters' club soared. However, any manager will tell you that one good League result wins nothing and so it was the results of other matches which indicated Dundee's consistency to the fans and the fact that they really did have a good chance that year. Early in the season, for example, the club played magnificently at Fir Park, Motherwell, to beat Bobby Ancell's ever-skilful side 4-2, and the week after the Ibrox result they fought tooth and nail to beat Raith Rovers 5-4 at Dens in a fantastic finish. Further, a first round Scottish Cup defeat at the hands of St Mirren, whilst temporarily shaking their confidence, served to focus their attention on the League challenge.

At Tannadice, Stewart Fraser was turning in some great performances with Yeats' successor Doug Smith, and was recognised by a Scottish League cap, but all eyes were fixed on the Dundee players and, ironically, United did them a good turn in March 1962 when they registered their first-ever victory (1-0) at Ibrox. Dundee FC then consolidated their position with a 2-1 away win at Tannadice on the holiday Monday, but the crucial matches took place on Wednesday 25 April. That night Aberdeen beat Rangers 1-0 at Pittodrie and when Liney saved a penalty at Dens in a 2-0 victory over St Mirren, it became known as "the night that turned the championship". Only fifteen players were used by Dundee FC in the entire season, the famous team: Liney; Hamilton and Cox (Capt.); Seith, Ure and Wishart; Smith, Penman, Cousin, Gilzean and Robertson; plus Craig Brown (6 games); Bobby Waddell (4); Alec Stuart (2) and George McGeachie (2). Five of them originally came from the general Tayside area.

Dundee FC met St Johnstone at Muirton in the final game of the season, knowing that victory would give them the flag and they won it in style, by three goals to nil (Gilzean 2, Penman). St Johnstone, unfortunately, were relegated as a result, but this could not dampen the enthusiasm of the Dundee fans and, coincidentally, Liverpool won the English Second Division Championship. It was brother Bob's team which was bound for Europe that year, however.

Dundee FC had travelled only occasionally abroad since the early 1920s, when William McIntosh took them to Spain.[2] George Anderson saw the value of such travel and took the club to Belgium in the late forties and to Turkey and the Middle East in the early fifties, but recent travel had been fairly restricted and Shankly made good use of an opportunity to test his side against European opposition by accepting an offer to play in a close-season tournament in New York (1962). Dundee's results were disappointing but the defence at least benefited from the experiment of playing to different systems. Shankly was not particularly happy with Pat Liney's form, however, and decided to buy another 'keeper, Bert Slater, who himself had lost his first team place with Liverpool.

In the first round of the European Cup (1962-63) Dundee FC drew FC Cologne, German champions, and one of the sides fancied to win the competition. Dundee's League Cup performances had been disappointing and no-one could have foreseen what was to happen in the first match, played at Dens on 5 September. Dundee lined up with their recognised side but with Slater in goal, and they proceeded to run up a 3-0 advantage before the German goalkeeper was injured in an innocuous clash with Cousin. At half-time, with the score 5-0, he was taken off suffering from concussion and Dundee eventually won by eight goals to one. This of course was an exhilarating result for Dundee fans and Scottish football for the match had not been a rough-house, but the rumblings from the German camp suggested they thought otherwise, and that the return might see a very different result "if, say, the Dundee goalkeeper was injured" — a quote actually attributed to the Cologne coach by the German newspapers.

It was unlikely that the man had the gift of second sight, but it was an ominous sign, and when the stretcher-bearers took up their position behind the Dundee FC goal in the return match at the Müngersdorf Stadium, the travelling support feared the worst. In an early attack Slater was deliberately kicked on the head and had to be replaced by Penman, although the goalkeeper refused to be taken to hospital and later resumed on the wing. Penman played well but had to face a penalty with the score at 4-0 and had that been converted, Cologne would probably have gone on to win. It was missed, however, and with Slater back in goal, Dundee finished the match 8-5 ahead on aggregate. But worse was to follow.

When it became obvious that their team could not overhaul the Dark Blues, hundreds of German fans encircled the pitch and in the absence of any police action, laid into the Dundee players, sometimes with chairs, as they tried to reach the dressing-rooms, some fifty yards away, at the end of the match.[3] It was despicable treatment and the Dundee FC board refused to attend the post-match reception.

In the second round their opponents were Sporting Club of Lisbon and from the first match, played away, they returned with a creditable 1-0 defeat. At Dens the crowd was 31,000 and with Ian Ure in great form at the back, the Dundee forwards had a field day, scoring four times without reply. United meantime, inaugurated their floodlights with a match against Rangers (9 November 1962) and Carlyle scored one of his "specials", but everything was riding on Dundee FC and Europe and in the next round they gave what was arguably their best-ever performance abroad.

On 6 March 1963, they visited the Belgian champions Anderlecht and confounded the soccer world with a 4-1 away victory, including two goals from Gilzean. The home match was therefore something of a formality but this was also won, by two goals to one and before a capacity 40,000 crowd.

The semi-finalists in the European Cup of 1963 were Benfica, also of Lisbon, AC Milan, Feyenoord of Rotterdam, and Dundee Football Club — an achievement which speaks for itself — and the Dark Blues drew Milan, with the first game to be played in the (more) fashionable Italian city. AC had players such as Rivera, Maldini and Trappatoni, and had knocked out English champions, Ipswich, in the second round, but the final was to be played at Wembley that year and Dundee knew that if they could surmount the semi-final hurdle, they would have a good chance of actually winning the Cup.

It was not to be, however. Captain Bobby Cox was injured and his place went to the young Alec Stuart and given that an all-out defensive

"Wha's that wi' Shug Robertson?"
Dundee FC players Hugh Robertson and George Ryden meet the Beatles,
Caird Hall, 1963.

(Courtesy: DC Thomson)

107

effort might be required in the first game, Hugh Robertson was replaced on the left-wing by the more versatile Doug Houston. In the first half, in spite of refereeing which denied the Dundee players any physical contact whatsoever, the team performed well and a Cousin header equalised an earlier goal from Sani. In the second-half, however, a combination of a barrage of flash bulbs blinding Dundee's attack whenever they were in front of goal, and a cross-ball game punishing their defence, led to the loss of four more goals.

It is always easy to blame biased refereeing or underhand tactics in such matches, but an incident some *five days* later illustrates the volatility of the Italian game at the time and the atmosphere in which it was often played. During a game between Naples and Modena the crowd rioted and smashed the posts. One person was killed and 89 injured. Fortunately, things were not so bad at Dens Park in the return match with Milan, which Dundee won 1-0, but Gilzean was sent off in the face of provocation and even Gordon Smith[4] was seen to retaliate once — a very rare sight indeed.

AC Milan went on to win the European Cup and Spurs the Cupwinners' Cup; United finished seventh in the Scottish League, two places above Dundee FC; and the "Swinging Sixties" made their first tentative moves with the Beatles and Christine Keeler rocking British youth and the Conservative government, respectively.

NOTES

1 — Cowie received no benefit game and his experience was later cited by Ian Ure as one of the reasons why he had to seek a transfer and more money.

2— Spanish results, 1923: 2-0 *v* Real Madrid; 3-0 and 1-0 *v* Valencia; 3-0 and 1-1 *v* Bilbao; 0-2 and 1-3 *v* Barcelona.

3 — Some British Servicemen stationed in Germany were at the match and came to the assistance of the Dundee players.

4 — Smith had now played in the European Cup for three different clubs, Hibs, Hearts and Dundee, a record.

15

IT HAD BEEN known since the late fifties that the future of British football teams in terms both of earning power and prestige lay in the European competitions, and these games also served to give players some idea of their individual standing in the international game. The Dundee FC players who made the greatest impression in Europe in the early sixties were Ian Ure and Alan Gilzean.

Ure had originally come from Ayr where he attended the rugby-playing Ayr Academy and so he was a late developer in football but his strong physique and aerial power marked him out as a defender of international class. The abolition of the maximum wage in England made it certain that his future lay south of the border. This was a time when a number of top-class Scottish players made that move and Ure's choice, following a brief dispute with Dundee FC (during which he attempted to claim unemployment benefit)[1] was Arsenal, then managed by Billy Wright. The fee was £62,500 and his replacement in the Dundee team was his understudy, George Ryden.

Gilzean, a Coupar Angus man like his nineteenth century namesakes, whose goalscoring feats[2] and heading skills in particular will always live with anyone fortunate enough to have seen them, played for Dundee FC for one more season but it was inevitable that he too would move, and he was transferred in December 1964 to Tottenham Hotspur for £72,500. His replacement was another outstanding footballer, only this time a ball-playing inside forward who seemed to have the ability to beat men in slow motion, Charlie Cooke, who came from Aberdeen FC for £30,000.

United, however, were not standing still at this time. Alternating

109

between an all-black and red and white "Arsenal" strip, they continued to consolidate their First Division status and most important, to stay in profit. Duncan Hutchison became chairman, succeeding Ernest Robertson. In the wider world, Peter Doig was elected Labour MP for Dundee West (Britain would have a Labour Government under Harold Wilson the following year) and, on 22 November 1963, President Kennedy was assassinated in Dallas.

Dundee FC reached the final of the Scottish Cup that season (1963-64) but lost by two late goals to Rangers in a 3-1 defeat. The team was Slater, Hamilton and Cox; Seith, Ryden and Stuart; Penman, Cousin, Cameron, Gilzean and Robertson; but as Rangers also won the League that year, the Dark Blues qualified for the 1964-65 European Cup Winners Cup.

Dundee's goalscorer in the final was new centre-forward Kenny "On the Spot" Cameron, who would later end up at Tannadice, first as a player and then as coach, and United also introduced some new faces around this time in goalkeeping rivals Donald McKay and Sandy Davie, utility player Benny Rooney and teenage forwards Ian Mitchell and Frank Munro. The Terrors also began to establish something of a hoodoo over their local rivals in derby games, but more of that later, for the main topic of interest at Tannadice as at Dens in the mid-1960s was the continent of Europe, only it was not in competition that United made their initial impact, but in the transfer market.

Following the example set by Hal Stewart[3] at Morton, the enterprising Jerry Kerr discovered that there was a pool of talent available in Scandinavia and, on account of local regulations governing professional football, at comparatively little cost. Kerr's first signing, and arguably his best, was a classy Swedish left-winger, Orjan Persson, who initially signed amateur forms. He was followed by fellow-countryman Lennart Wing and Danes, Finn Dossing, Mogens Berg and Finn Seemann. The Scandinavians were both popular and successful as players. On 11 September 1965, Dossing scored a hat-trick in a 5-0 United victory over Dundee at Dens and Persson eventually moved to Rangers with whom he also enjoyed success.

In the European Cup Winners Cup Dundee FC drew 2-2 with Zaragossa at Dens but lost 4-3 on aggregate and Shankly saw this result as demonstrating that he had achieved all he could for Dundee Football Club. He now moved on to manage Hibs, replacing Jock Stein who had gone to Celtic, but left his successor Bobby Ancell some fine

Dundee United 1966/67.
Back Row: Berg, Mitchell, McKay, McAlpine, Davie, Munro, Thomson.
Middle Row: Modre, Briggs, Carroll, Gillespie, McLeish, Smith, Wing.
Front Row: Persson, Dick, McFall, Dossing, Stewart, Neilson, Hainey.

(Courtesy: DC Thomson)

young players including Ally Donaldson, Steve Murray, Alec Totten, George Stewart and Jocky Scott.

Bobby Seith was now appointed coach at Dens; Celtic's first non-Catholic manager won the Scottish Cup for them at his first attempt; another provincial side, Kilmarnock, won the League (1964-65); United beat Dundee FC twice in the Summer Cup and reached the final only to lose to Motherwell on aggregate;[4] Hugh Robertson went to Dunfermline Athletic and became the first Scot to play in all three European tournaments; and Scotland failed to qualify for the 1966 World Cup Finals.

In December 1965, Dundee FC signed Jim Mclean, the Clyde inside-forward. Originally from Larkhall, McLean was one of three footballing brothers who enjoyed varying success as players but who, like the Shankly brothers before them, would become better-known as managers. At the turn of the year United were in fourth place in the First Division, their best mid-term showing to date, and they finished the season in fifth position, thus qualifying for a place in the Inter-

Cities Fairs Cup. Dundee FC finished ninth and when Charlie Cooke announced that he wished to break his contract with the club (he eventually went to Chelsea for £72,000) the well-known Scots football journalist Hugh Taylor was moved to voice his disgust at the player's decision in the *Daily Record*.

In an astonishing article he first said that had he been a Dundee fan, he would now switch his allegiance to Tannadice and he followed this up with the pronouncement that he was fed up with those who carped at the success of Rangers and Celtic. The Old Firm, he opined, were "entitled to rule Scottish soccer" because they "kept it alive". He did get one thing right when he forecast that Dundee FC by transferring their star players would now suffer at the turnstiles and, to my knowledge, he was the first to coin the term "The New Firm" referring to Tommy Docherty's young Scotland team of 1971. But that's about all.

Dundee FC could not possibly have held on to their star players and to some extent were victims of their own success. How they invested the (net) quarter of a million pounds received for Brown, Gabriel, Ure, Gilzean and Cooke, however, might have stood closer scrutiny.

In any event, it was now United's turn to savour European glory for the first time. They had got their chance in the Fairs Cup as a result of an extension of the Scottish representation to three clubs, and Kerr took them to Scandinavia for a close-season preparation. Even the most optimistic fan, however, could not have anticipated the pay-off, for in the very first round they drew the holders Barcelona, with the first game to be played in Spain.

England had won the World Cup that year with a 4-3-3 formation and it was this which Kerr deployed with brilliant success. On 26 October 1966, in their first-ever competitive European match, they beat Barcelona 2-1 (away) with goals from Billy Hainey and Finn Seemann (penalty). In the return game Ian Mitchell opened for United and the ex-Thistle striker Hainey made it two from a speculative effort. The away result was hailed as "the best ever . . . achieved by a Scottish side abroad" and the aggregate victory, said the *Record*, would "ring around Europe". It would not be for the last time.[5]

United were in a particularly healthy condition at this time with Taypools worth £30,000 a year to them, and gates were rising at Tannadice whilst they fell elsewhere. In the second round they drew another big name in Juventus of Turin and in the first (away) leg

Seemann almost scored in the first minute. Disaster struck in the second-half, however, and the game was lost 3-0. At Tannadice the score was 1-0 for United.

This was the season (1966-67) in which Celtic would win the European Cup but there was almost equal drama on the domestic front. Bob Seith became trainer-coach of Rangers in December 1966, but almost before he had time to take off his Dundee FC blazer, Rangers had suffered one of the worst results in their history going down 1-0 (away) to Jock Wallace's team, Berwick Rangers, in the first round of the Scottish Cup. Heads were bound to roll and besides players George McLean and Jim Forest (McLean came to Dundee in part exchange for Andy Penman), manager Scot Symon also got "the boot" later that year in spite of the fact that he had taken them to the final of the Cup Winners Cup (1967). Seith then resigned in protest, saying that he "no longer wished to be part of an organisation which can treat a loyal servant so badly".

Dundee United beat Celtic home and away in the Celts' glory season, the only club to do so; Alex Ferguson became the star of his club, Dunfermline; and Davie White when appointed the new manager of Rangers signed that striker for the Light Blues. Orjan Persson was then also transferred to Rangers, with Davy Wilson and Wilson Wood coming to Tannadice.

By a quirky ruling Dundee FC, who finished sixth in the League (United were eighth) were given a place in the 1967-68 Fairs Cup — only one representative could come from each city and this debarred Clyde — and in the first round they defeated DWS Amsterdam 3-2 on aggregate with Jim McLean scoring two in the home tie.[6]

Dundee FC reached the final of the League Cup in 1967 but lost two goals to Celtic in the first eleven minutes and in spite of a good performance by George McLean, went down 5-3 (G McLean 2, J McLean). They lined up: Arrol; R Wilson and Houston; Murray, Stewart and Stuart; Campbell,[7] J McLean, and S Wilson;[7] G McLean and Bryce.

In the second round of the Fairs Cup Dundee FC beat Royal Liege 3-1 at Dens and scored a remarkable 4-1 away victory with George McLean getting all four. McLean, like Walter Carlyle, was a Saint one day and a Sinner the next, but was another who always gave at least entertainment value for money. Bobby Seith now went to manage Preston; Bob Shankly's Hibs side included Peter Cormack, Pat Stanton and Colin Stein; and the popular press reported that Scotland was living in an "age of violence". There had apparently been 49 murders in ten months in the country and the main recipient of the sensational reporting was one James "Baby Face" Boyle, aged twenty-four, from Gorbals. In fact there was a great deal of social upheaval and violence throughout the world at this time with the Vietnam war at its height, the assassination of Martin Luther King and Bobby Kennedy in America and the Russian invasion of Czechoslovakia.

In the quarter-finals of the European Fairs Cup Dundee FC defeated FC Zurich 1-0 in both matches and Don Revie's fine Leeds United team put out Hibs, so the scene was set for an all British semi-final. Reaching that stage was a really fine achievement for Dundee — "Europe's Ghost Team" as they were described — but the times had changed as far as the fans were concerned. Only 41,000 in total watched the first three home ties and the old enthusiasm could not be summoned. Away goals also now counted double in this tournament and a Paul Madeley counter, although equalised by Bobby Wilson, virtually saw Leeds through. The Yorkshire club won the return tie 1-0 and went on to win the competition.

Frank Munro went to Aberdeen; Doug Smith missed his first game in four and a half years; and Denis Gillespie was described as the best (fully) uncapped player in Scotland. Bobby Ancell "blooded" two young strikers, John Duncan and Roddy Georgeson and, feeling that a younger man should also be in the manager's chair, stepped down himself in favour of John Prentice in October 1969. Jim McLean was then transferred to Kilmarnock and men walked on the moon. The two events were unconnected, however.

NOTES

1 — Three Dundee FC players, Marsh, McNab and Gilmour, had also sought recourse to Social Security in 1932, before the dispute was settled.

2 — Gilzean broke Alec Stott's club goalscoring record by scoring 53 goals in season 1963-64.

3 — Stewart was a Dundonian who had assisted George Anderson in a personal capacity.

4 — Motherwell 3 United 1; United 1 Motherwell 0.

5 — United's team in Barcelona was: Davie; Miller and Briggs; Neilson, Smith and

Wing; Seeman, Hainey, Mitchell, Gillespie and Persson.

6 — In domestic competition Dundee FC were said by the *Daily Record* to be "dreadfully disappointing" in a match against United and "unlikely to challenge Celtic". It is revealing that the prospect of United challenging Celtic was not even considered by the Glasgow press, as recently as this.

7 — Billy Campbell and Sammy Wilson were both capped by N. Ireland and Bobby Wilson by the Scottish League. Alec Bryce came from Clyde and John Arrol from Stirling Albion.

16

JOHN PRENTICE had had an eventful career in football. As a player he captained the Scottish Cup-winning Falkirk side in 1957 and as a manager he was briefly in charge of the Scotland team before being sacked for investigating the possibility of another job in Canada. His first season at Dens, however, will probably only be remembered for the transfer of Jim McLean to Kilmarnock where he teamed up with younger brother, Tommy. Dundee finished tenth that year and United a most creditable fifth, with Kenny Cameron the first United player to top the scoring charts since Johnny Coyle.

The following season United drew Newcastle United in the first round of the Fairs Cup and in spite of two great performances by Alec Reid, went down 2-1 at home and 1-0 away, but the Tangerines[1] maintained their League position and Dundee FC were not far behind. The Dark Blues also reached the semi-final of the Scottish Cup but went out 2-1 to a great Celtic team who then beat Leeds United on the way to their second European Cup Final (which they lost 2-1 to Feyenoord).

With Richard Nixon as President the Americans now extended the Vietnam War in Cambodia; Paul McCartney announced the break-up of the Beatles; and Aberdeen won the Scottish Cup with Dundonian Davie Robb and ex-Dundee FC player Derek McKay playing prominent parts. Edward Heath's Tories formed a Government; United's talented wing-half or inside-forward Jim Henry was capped by the Scottish League against the league of Ireland; and Jim McLean returned to Dens as first-team coach (April, 1970) on the understanding that he would not appear for them as a player.

In the 1970-71 Fairs Cup, United drew Grasshoppers of Zurich in the first round and a 3-2 victory at home was enough to see them through. In the second round they faced Sparta of Prague and in the first (away) game Donald McKay suffered a pulled muscle. "On you go, son," was Jerry Kerr's instruction to the young Hamish McAlpine, a goalkeeper whose father had played for Dundee FC, and who had signed from North End some four years earlier. The game was lost 3-1 and when only a 1-0 victory was recorded at Tannadice the *Daily Record* attributed the aggregate defeat to the substitution. More would be heard of McAlpine, however.

In season 1970-71, Dundee FC fared much better. They were in sixth place at the "halfway" mark (United were thirteenth and this was also the season of the Ibrox disaster, when sixty-six people died and 103 were injured when railings collapsed on a stairway at the end

Dundee FC July 1971.
Back Row: R Wilson, Phillip, Hewitt, Donaldson, Stewart, Johnston,
Jim McLean (Coach).
Middle Row: John Prentice (Manager), Robinson, I Scott, Steele, Selway,
Lambie, Maurice Friel (Physio).
Front Row: Bryce, Duncan, Kinninmouth, Houston, Wallace, J Scott,
J Wilson.
(Courtesy: DC Thomson)

117

of the New Year Rangers-Celtic match) and qualified for Europe in spite of yet another home defeat from United. The Terrors were now unbeaten at Dens for nine years but changes were on the way, for McLean was beginning to make his presence felt as a hard worker and disciplinarian and, following a successful pre-season tour of France and Belgium, Dundee FC began the 1971-72 season brightly, including a long-awaited win over United at Dens. The final score was 6-4 to the Dark Blues and Mclean's after-match comment was particularly revealing: "At 5-1 up," he said, "we had a tremendous chance of a big win to make up for all the years we couldn't beat United." There is no doubt where his loyalties lay at this time and in the short time he was at Dens as coach his results spoke for themselves. In the revamped Fairs Cup (1971-72) — the European Union or UEFA Cup — Dundee beat Academisk (Denmark) 4-2 (home) and 1-0 (away) in the first round. In the second round they faced their old rivals FC Cologne and although they lost 2-1 in Germany, a Duncan hat-trick saw them through 4-2 at Dens. Remarkably they now drew AC Milan and once again the Italians proved to be the stumbling block. In Milan, Dundee lost 3-0 and in spite of a fantastic performance at Dens Park they went down 3-2 on aggregate (Wallace and Duncan scored at Dens). The Dundee FC team was: Hewitt; R Wilson and Houston; Steele, Phillip and Stewart; Duncan, Lambie, Wallace, J Scott and J Wilson. "Dundee Football Club," said Jock Stein, "played better against Milan than any other Scottish team, and that includes Celtic." But even a tribute as eloquent as this could not produce a result and it is results (and clichés!) which count in this game.

Some Scottish football clubs suddenly now appeared to wake up to a crisis and Dundee were one. Attendances had been steadily falling throughout football since the fifties but the respective figures for Dundee FC's campaigns in 1963 and 1971 say it all. In 1963 the game at Dens against AC Milan was watched by 40,000 people. The equivalent tie in 1971 drew only 15,000 and indeed the *combined* attendances for all three 1971 games just managed to pass the 40,000 mark. Tournaments such as the UEFA Cup and Texaco Cup were designed to provide mid-table clubs with attractive games, but the plan did not appear to be working and something had to give. Events in the footballing history of the City of Dundee now took a momentous turn.

On 11 November 1971 Dundee United had called a press conference for the first time in their history to announce that Jerry Kerr —

Scotland's longest serving manager with twelve-and-a-half years' service — had resigned as team manager to take up the position of general manager at the club. The seemingly indestructible Kerr had taken ill at a match against Hibs and it was obvious the barracking he was receiving from some fans as a result of United's poor start to the season was taking its toll. One of the candidates for the job was Davie White, the ex-Rangers manager who had been replaced at Ibrox by Willie Waddell, but before an appointment could be made the spotlight returned to Dens where John Prentice also seemed poised to make a statement. Prentice's utterances following the first Milan game had been increasingly pessimistic ("What's the point? "What's the future of the game in Scotland?") and when his home in Barnhill was seen to be advertised for sale, it was obvious he planned to go. What happened next, however, would have taxed the imagination of a soap opera scriptwriter.

Chairman James Gellatly made the first move by accepting Prentice's resignation and announcing it to the Press. Simultaneously he announced that Prentice's successor would be none other than Davie White and the fact that White had been a player under Prentice at Clyde suggests that he was recommended for the Dundee job by his former boss. Now this meant that Jim McLean as Dundee FC coach was overlooked for the manager's job and whether he expected this can only be gauged from the news the following day that the new *United* manager was — Jim McLean. Here was one man who was quite sure not only that football had a future, but that he was going to play a major part in it.[2]

"It could mean the start of a new era for the club," said the *Courier* prophetically of United's new manager, and again it was emphasised that McLean would have full control of the playing side while Kerr looked after the administration. His first pool was McAlpine; Rolland, Mollison, J Cameron, W Smith, D Smith, Markland, Henry Traynor, Copland, K Cameron, Gordon and Reid (Ian Mitchell,[3] Billy Gray, Joe Watson and Morris Stevenson were injured) and his first post-match assessment following a 2-2 home draw with Ayr United was, "Not good enough". It was a cry which would often be heard from the manager's office.

Jim Steele, Dundee's skilled, if somewhat agricultural midfield player, now went to Southampton for £80,000 — and later won an FA Cup Winner's medal;[4] Tommy Gemmell left Celtic for Nottingham

Forest, and another fine club servant, Ronnie Yeats, left Liverpool for Tranmere Rovers. "No player in the history of the Liverpool club," said Bill Shankly, "has given greater service than Yeats . . . he proved the very foundation of our tremendous success and I cannot pay him too great a tribute."

The *Courier* also let slip something which might be regarded as a little bias when, in describing the United fans' heckling of Jim Steele, remarked, "the frustrated terracing 'Arabs' mounted a continuing offensive".[5]

How that kind of thing goes down in the Tannadice boardroom can best be described as a kind of conspiracy theory but it did not put McLean off his stride for, having outlined his philosophy of "winning, but winning well" and giving "entertainment value", he got down to a veritable orgy of football management. The cornerstone of his managerial career was to be a youth policy — initially to bring down the average age of the team — and his first list of "S" form signings makes interesting reading, for not only does it contain the name of David Narey (St Johns) but also that of Cameron Fraser (Linlathen). The youngsters of course required assistance from older players as well as from management and once again the value of men such as Doug Smith and Denis Gillespie was in evidence in the transitional period. But McLean also made some astute moves in the transfer market, selling Alan Gordon (to Hibs for £12,000) and buying George Fleming (from Hearts, £7,000), Pat Gardner (from Dunfermline, £4,500) and Archie Knox (from St Mirren, £3,000). Frank Kopel was then picked up as a free transfer from Blackburn Rovers and McLean's commendable desire to build from within the community was further underlined when he insisted that *all* players must live in Dundee and district.

Davie White was also getting some change at Dens Park where Duncan, Wallace and Jocky Scott were linking up well, but "on the ground" McLean was having it all his own way. Twenty-two young players showed their paces at Tannadice in McLean's first six weeks and mostly locals, whereas most of Dundee's young signings came from other parts of the country. They did have one notable success, however, when in July 1972 an Edinburgh youngster named Gordon Strachan signed for Dundee FC on an 'S' form.[6]

Dundee FC finished fifth and United ninth at the end of the first four months under new management but both clubs were attracting poor crowds and their problems were compounded by the growing presence of the "football hooligan". Often victims of unemployment or broken homes, young rowdies discovered they could bring attention to themselves by behaving violently at football matches and Dundee FC somehow managed to attract a particularly malevolent crew who chose to imitate the hooligan element of the Rangers support and sing Orange and Loyalist songs. This was particularly inappropriate because, as explained earlier, Dundee United had come into being in part to repudiate sectarianism and many of the young Dundee fans were themselves Catholics, who now could be found in the Dens Road enclosure mindlessly singing "No Surrender" and "God Save the Queen"! Willie Waddell of Rangers spoke out against his "unruly mobs" at this time but to date no such public statement has been heard from a Dundee FC chairman.

Bobby Seith now became manager of Hearts; Peter Ustinov was reaching the end of his term as the Rector of the University of Dundee; and Jim McLean picked up where Jerry Kerr had left off, beating Dundee 2-1 at Tannadice.

United now went to the top of the league and stayed there for seven games and their final position of seventh (1972-73) was a significant improvement for McLean's first season. Dundee FC, however, went two better (fifth place), in part due to the performance of Scotland's top goalscorer, John Duncan (40 goals), and when the young forward scored two against the English League it became a question of *when* he would move to an English club rather than *if*. In fact, the transfer, to Tottenham Hotspur for £140,000, did not go through until October 1974, by which time United themselves had found a goalscoring ace and Duncan had helped Dundee FC win another trophy.

NOTES

1 — United changed to an all-Tangerine strip in 1969.

2 — One casualty of the merry-go-round was Doug Cowie, who had been appointed coach to United in 1966. He would later be re-employed, however.

3 — Ian Mitchell was transferred to Newcastle United in season 1969-70 for £50,000. He did not establish himself in the first team, however, and returned, just before McLean arrived, in exchange of Alec Reid.

4 — Steele teamed up at Southampton with Jimmy Gabriel.

5 — The "Arabs" was a name given to United and their fans by their Dundee rivals when in the harsh winter of 1963 they burned ice — and the grass — from the pitch and put down sand to make the pitch playable.

6 — Clubs were limited to 20 "S" signings, not more than 10 in each age group 13-14 and 14-15.

17

ANDY GRAY, a United "S" form signing from Drumchapel, was the first young "star" to emerge from Jim McLean's galaxy. Capped by Scotland's Schoolboys, Juveniles, Amateur Youth and Professional Youth teams, the powerful young centre-forward was a terrific "scoop" for scout Maurice Friel[1] and was obviously won over by McLean's promise of an early chance of first-team football. He made his debut against East Fife in August 1973 and teamed up alongside club stalwarts like Sandy Davie, who had returned from a spell in English football[2] and Andy Rolland.

Graham Payne (St Columba's) was the next youth to be called into the first team squad and McLean's policy contrasted sharply with that of White who seemed to concentrate his efforts on the transfer market and even the free transfer market whence came Tommy Gemmell. In fairness, however, White put together a successful team more quickly than did McLean and at least one free-transfer man, goalkeeper Thompson Allan, was a great signing for the club. In the 1973 League Cup Dundee FC qualified from Section 3, which included Hearts, St Johnstone and Partick Thistle. Defender Ian Phillip who had gone to Crystal Palace the previous season for £112,000 returned to Dens for £60,000 and Dundee also tried to bring back Steve Murray from Aberdeen. The side had acquired a certain rhythm and defeated Clyde 3-2 on aggregate in the next round. An experimental offside rule was used in the competition that year but it had no effect on Tommy Gemmell's foraging style and one of his long-range specials against Kilmarnock put Dundee FC into the final.

The Scottish League Cup Final played at Hampden Park on

Saturday 15 December 1973 took place in most peculiar circumstances. The country was in the middle of a fuel crisis which, compounded by an overtime ban by the miners and railwaymen, had led industry to the brink of a three-day week. In order to conserve power, the game between Dundee FC and Celtic kicked off early and with generators standing by. Further, it was snowing in the Glasgow area and this deterred a number of Dundee fans (Att. 30,000) but happily for them it did not deter Gordon Wallace who in the 75th minute chested down a Bobby Wilson free-kick in the penalty area, and smacked it into the left-hand corner of the Celtic net. White did not think the game should have taken place but was doubtless glad it did. The Dundee FC team was: Allan; Wilson and Gemmell; Ford, Stewart and Phillip; Duncan, Robinson, Wallace, J Scott and Lambie. Subs: Johnston and I Scott.

The victory came as a great boost to Dundee FC who had lost their unbeaten European home record earlier in the season to FC Twente Entschede (1-3; 2-4 away) in the UEFA Cup and United, too, received something of a morale boost with a couple of great aggregate victories against English opposition in the Texaco Cup. Sheffield United were despatched in the first round (0-0 away; 2-0 home), Leicester City in the second (1-1 away; 1-0 home) and only an away disaster prevented them from overcoming Newcastle United in the third round (2-0 home; 1-4 away). Midfielder Jim Henry[3] was the architect of victory in these games and with Gray established in the first team and Narey, Payne and John Holt in the reserves, McLean was moved to comment, "I firmly believe that here at Tannadice we have a group of youngsters that any manager North or South of the border would be proud to be connected with."

Dundee FC began the year 1974 with a 2-1 victory over United at Tannadice and then embarked upon a remarkable Scottish Cup campaign which became known as their "Month of Sundays", as their ties were played on Sundays that season. Aberdeen went down 2-0 at Pittodrie; Rangers (now managed by Jock Wallace) lost 3-0 at Ibrox and, following a 3-3 draw with Hibs at Easter Road in the fifth round, Dundee FC pulled 30,000 fans to the Wednesday replay at Dens. The fans were obviously still there if the attraction was right and when Dundee FC won 3-0, Jim McLean described them as "the best team in Scotland". Yet again, they failed to live up to it, however, going down 1-0 to Celtic in the semi-final.

Now, almost unnoticed in the light of Dundee's remarkable series of

Dundee FC at the civic reception to mark their League Cup victory 1973/74.
Back Row: J Scott, R Wilson, Lambie, J Wilson, Duncan, Wallace, Phillip,
Johnston, E Ferguson (Physio), T Arnot (Scout), I Scott, J Toner (Scout),
Stewart, H Robertson (Coach), Ford.
Front Row: W K Fitzgerald, T Gemmell, Lord Provost Tom Moore, D White
(Manager), H Davis (Coach).

(Courtesy: DC Thomson)

results United, too, had reached the semis beating Airdrie, Morton and Dunfermline in a replay, and in the semi-final replay, Andy Gray scored the winner in a 3-2 victory over Hearts (the first game was drawn 1-1). It was United's first "real" Scottish Cup Final and a great reward for club servants like Doug Smith. The game was Sandy Davie's last for United before he emigrated and a great performance meant it was no fault of his that the Jute City missed out on a cup "double" that season. United were outplayed by Celtic, and lost 3-0, but they did qualify for the European Cup Winners Cup. The United team was: Davie; Gardner and Kopel, Copland, D Smith and W Smith, Payne, Knox, Gray, Fleming and Houston.[4] Subs: Traynor and Rolland.

The Terrors also had two unusual "supporters" at the final — Dundee FC Director Ian Gellatly who claimed that Dundonians were

125

all on the same side on such a day, and Billy Connolly, the Scottish comedian who was beginning to break through in a big way in 1974 and who claimed divided loyalty because of the support he had received over the years from the Dundee Folk Club.

Meanwhile, the cost of Ninewells Hospital had soared to twenty-four and a half million; the activities of ex-Provost Tom Moore, Bailie J L Stewart and Councillor Harry Dickson were coming under increasing scrutiny and Murdoch Wallace Jnr, proprietor of the JM Ballroom now also took over its traditional rival, the Palais, in South Tay Street. Dundee finished fifth in the League and United eighth; Willie Ormond had his finest hour at the World Cup in Germany when his Scotland team outplayed Brazil and failed to qualify from their section on goal average (Thomson Allan made the squad); David Narey began to establish himself in the United first-team (as offers began coming in for Andy Gray); and another star was born when sixteen-year-old Paul Sturrock was named in the United first team pool in September 1974.

McLean was obviously warming to the task by now and appealed for bigger gates which he said would enable him "to bring honour to the City of Dundee". In the Cup Winners' Cup United beat Jiul Petrosani (Rumania) in the first round 3-2 on aggregate, but went out 1-0 on aggregate to Bursapor after another long journey, this time to Turkey. Dundee went out of the UEFA Cup 5-2 on aggregate to RWD Amsterdam in the first round.

However, the clubs had quite a lot on their plate on the domestic front that year for the much-discussed Premier League was to become a reality the following season (1975-76) and the ten-club Premier Division was to be composed of the top ten teams of the First Division. Again White looked to the tranfer market, bringing ex-United man Alan Gordon to Dens for £15,000, and United did likewise, signing the nineteen-year-old Hamilton striker, Paul Hegarty, for £40,000. United as usual, however, also had youngsters coming through at the same time. Centre-forward David Dodds, for example, was a provisional signing by now and he would soon be followed by Derek Addison and Raymond Stewart, and with United in fourth place in the League, McLean wisely used the "safety net" of guaranteed Premier League status to introduce new young players.

Another young Dundonian, however, Robbie MacIntosh (24), drummer with the Average White Band, had *his* life cut tragically short when he was given heroin at a party in America, which the group was about to conquer.

NOTES

1 — The former Dundee FC Physiotherapist.

2 — Donald McKay was freed by Jim McLean and moved first to Southend United.

3 — Henry, a local boy, later moved to Fulham, Aberdeen and Forfar. But for protracted illness he might have done even better in the game.

4 — Houston was the ex-Dundee FC player who had gone to Ibrox for £30,000, then came to Tannadice for £20,000. Jackie Copland was signed by Jerry Kerr from Stranraer for £10,000 in 1970. Walter Smith would later become McLean's right-hand man.

18

THE SCOTTISH PREMIER League was inaugurated in 1975 and consisted of the following sides: Rangers, Hibs, Celtic, Dundee United, Aberdeen, Dundee FC, Ayr United, Hearts, St Johnstone and Motherwell. (This was the order in which the first ten clubs finished the previous season. The next sixteen formed the First Division and the final sixteen the Second Division).

Neither Dundee FC nor United qualified for the League Cup, although Gordon Strachan made a notable breakthrough to the Dundee FC first team; Britain voted to join the Common Market; and East End Park, Dunfermline, sold the dearest pies in Scottish football (they were good though, as I remember). Dundee FC captain Bobby Ford scored the first goal of the Premier League; war was declared on football hooligans by Sports Minister Denis Howell; and once again violence was not confined to a particular minority. Dundee's Lord Provost, for example, Mr Charles Farquhar, was charged with assault following an incident at Camperdown Golf Club in September, 1975.

Andy Gray was transferred to Aston Villa for £110,000[1] — "McLean must go" chanted the fans; Jocky Scott went to Aberdeen for £15,000; and McLean's master plan was taken a stage further as his young squad continued to pick up regular European experience.

In the first round of the UEFA Cup, United beat Keflavik of Iceland 2-0 (away) and 4-0 (home) but in the second round they went down 2-1 at home in the first game against FC Porto. "They let the fans down," said McLean and indeed this "bad team" then put United out in a 3-2 aggregate. Tom McAdam was signed from Dumbarton for £40,000 in another attempt by McLean to find a finisher and this would be his problem position for some time before a solution was found from within the ranks.

At the turn of the year (1976), Dundee were seventh and United ninth out of ten, but whilst United gained ground Dundee began to lose their position and on completion of their programme, had 32 points from 36 games. Ayr United and Dundee United both had 31 points from 35 games and so when the Ayr team beat Motherwell in a mid-week game it meant one of the Dundee clubs must go down following United's last match at Ibrox. In that game McAlpine took and missed a penalty but otherwise played well to gain a 0-0 draw which meant it was Dundee Football Club which was relegated, for the first time in thirty-eight years.

Relegation in 1976 marked the beginning of a nightmare for Dundee FC and Jim McLean was sympathetic. "The penalty for failure is too great," he complained and favoured a twelve-team division. McLean also said at a later date that the Premier League had come one season too early for United. It almost came too early for Aberdeen as well for, as Dundee FC began to visit places like Hamilton and Montrose in the new season, United and Aberdeen — the two clubs which had finished

Andy Gray (bottom left) in typical action.

(Courtesy: DC Thomson)

129

directly above them — now raced to the top of the Premier League.

Doug Smith retired after 587 matches and no bookings — a fantastic record for a central defender at this time; Dundee FC, reckoning that relegation would cost them £100,000 per season, became agents for Rangers Pools; and Rangers themselves ran into another storm when their fans rioted during a game with Aston Villa. The following week General Manager Willie Waddell declared that in future there would no longer be religious barriers at Ibrox — although to this day the actual number of Catholics signed can be counted on one finger.[2] The next Saturday the Rangers fans stayed away in droves and those who did attend sang ditties like "You can stick your Fenian players . . .". When Jock Wallace on his return to Ibrox in 1983 remarked that "no-one spoke about sectarianism when he was winning Trebles" (Rangers won the Treble in 1975-76), his memory failed him somewhat.

Another manager who was facing a problem was Jerry Kerr who by this time had moved to Forfar Athletic with less than spectacular results. In what was an uncharacteristically distasteful episode, Kerr had been forced out at Tannadice in 1972 and failed to recover his touch after two years at Forfar (1974-76). He was succeeded at Forfar by Archie Knox, and later worked with Dundee FC.

David Narey was now the lynch-pin of the United defence and Gordon Wallace had crossed the road to lead the Tangerine attack; punk rock had arrived and the Sex Pistols were banned from appearing at the Caird Hall; and Jimmy Carter was the new American President. Britain also had a new leader, for Harold Wilson who had led his Labour Party to victory (twice) in 1974 now handed over the reins to Jim Callaghan; and football pundits on the west coast were also beginning to get a whiff of the wind of change as United and Aberdeen began to get results regularly on their territory.

Davie White, unfortunately, was not so lucky and resigned when he failed to get Dundee FC back into the Premier League in one season. His replacement was his League Cup-winning skipper — Tommy Gemmell — who for all his playing years had no coaching experience and did not apply for the job. The wisdom of the board's choice was soon to be tested.

One of Gemmell's ex-teammates, Billy McNeill, now became manager of Aberdeen in succession to Ally McLeod and another, Jimmy Johnstone, signed up as a player with "Big Tam" at Dens. The latter move was not a success, however, although Dundee began well with Gordon Strachan as captain. Over at Tannadice three more names were figuring on McLean's teamsheets, Ralph Milne and Derek Stark in the reserves, and Billy Kirkwood in the first team. Another Dundee FC player and "cap", Bobby Robinson, crossed the road in exchange for Billy Williamson plus £20,000; another striker John Bourke came to United from Dumbarton, while McAdam went to Celtic; and another rock star — this time one of the greatest, Elvis Presley — succumbed to the ravages of drugs. KB Copenhagen put United out of the UEFA Cup 3-1 on aggregate; McLean condemned drunken hooligans;and Dundee FC looked to have picked up two good youngsters in Ian Redford and the younger Ian Ferguson. The hope of rearing their own team like United, however, suffered a setback when Gemmell accepted a £50,000 bid plus Jim Shirra from Aberdeen for a young man who would go on to become one of the greatest players in the Scottish game, Gordon Strachan.

Liverpool, who had signed Kenny Dalglish from Celtic, watched Graham Payne, but he didn't go; Newcastle watched and bid for David Narey — he didn't go either; and Donald McKay the ex-United goalkeeper now at Bristol City as coach, was offered a similar position in Aslborg in Denmark. He did go.

Dundee FC failed once again to get promotion (1978) and Scotland suffered their greatest humiliation in Argentina. One consolation for United at least was that three of their players, Narey, Hegarty and Payne, made the World Cup 40 and their third place in the Premier League put them comfortably into Europe again. Standard Liege, just as comfortably, put them out, unfortunately, but Jim McLean's "education" was now nearing completion.

Billy McNeill became manager of Celtic and was replaced at Aberdeen by ex-St Mirren boss Alex Ferguson; Jock Stein went to Leeds United, then took on the Scotland job; and Jock Wallace, having won another Treble, left Ibrox suddenly, proclaiming that he would never reveal the reason why. Perhaps the fact that the in-demand David Narey went to St John's Secondary School in Johnston Avenue had something to do with it.

NOTES

1 — Gray had scored 40 goals in 96 games for United, and he would later be transferred to Wolves for a staggering one and a half million pounds. He was also the

English players' "Player of the Year" in his first season with Aston Villa.

2 — Rangers actually signed a Catholic in the 1950s and he was a Dundonian, Larry Blyth.

19

DAVID NAREY, a central defender or midfield player and an out-standing, instinctive reader of a game, was the first Dundee United player to receive a full Scotland cap. When he played his first full game against Portugal in November 1978 the Lion Rampant was hoisted over Tannadice. The club topped the Premier League at the time and Dundee FC were top of the First Division, and although the Dark Blues looked to be geared towards promotion as an end in itself they won their championship (1978-79) in an exciting climax and saved the club from financial disaster. Dundee FC from: Donaldson, Barr, Millar, Schaedler, Watson, Glennie, Shirra, Williamson, McLaren, Pirie, Sinclair, Murphy, Caldwell, McGhee, Redford and Lamb. Billy Pirie and Ian Redford were prolific goalscorers for the club.

Margaret Thatcher became Prime Minister and Gordon Wilson retained his seat in Dundee East for SNP, although his majority was cut by the Labour candidate, former UCS shop steward, Jimmy Reid; United toured Japan and Hamish McAlpine was sent home prior to the "Japan Cup Final" in which United went down 2-0 to Spurs; Jim McLean signed a new five-year contract despite another offer for his services, this time from Toronto Metros; and he then signed Willie Pettigrew the Motherwell centre-forward for £100,000. McAlpine was suspended and temporarily replaced by Peter Bonetti, the ex-Chelsea goalkeeper[1] who had moved his family from London to Mull. But you can't keep a good man down and the differences were soon patched up.

Dundee's George Stewart (£37,000) followed clubmate Bobby Hutchinson (£20,000) to Hibs and given that another £30,000 had been received from Sheffield United the previous year for young centre-half John McPhail, Dundee FC were continuing to do quite well in the transfer market. The players who remained, however, were not suitably prepared for the Premier League and the team went down again, in 1980.

Season 1979-80, however, will be remembered by the citizens of Dundee for another reason. This was the year United won their first major trophy. The club did not begin very cleverly in the League but in what was their seventh European campaign they had a good victory over Anderlecht in the first round of the UEFA Cup (0-0 home; 1-0 away, a Kopel "super goal"). In the second round they met Diosgyori Miskolc of Rumania — a club whose name no-one could pronounce comfortably except Mary Marquis — and United were also uncomfortable on the park, losing 1-0 at home and 3-1 away. The club was now on the march, however, and in October 1979 they paid a record fee for Chelsea's Scottish midfielder, Eamonn Bannon. The money had regrettably come from the £400,000 transfer of twenty-year-old full-back Raymond Stewart to West Ham but the deal paid off almost immediately, for within a month United had reached the sponsored final of the Bell's League Cup where they met east coast neighbours Aberdeen.

Results in earlier rounds were: second round — Airdrie 2 United 1, United 2 Airdrie 0; third round — Q. Park 0 United 3, United 2 Q. Park 1; fourth round — United 0 Raith Rovers 0, Raith Rovers 0 United 1; Semi-final — United 6 Hamilton 2.

The first game at Hampden was drawn 0-0 after extra-time but when the replay was scheduled for Dens Park, United's hopes were high. United fielded: McAlpine; Stark, Kopel, Phillip,[2] Hegarty, Narey, Bannon, Sturrock, Pettigrew, Holt and Kirkwood. Aberdeen lined up: Clark; Kennedy, Rougvie, McLeish, Garner, Miller, Strachan, Archibald, McGhee, McMaster and Scanlon. Payne was left on the bench owing to the heavy conditions, but second half goals from Pettigrew (2) and Sturrock brought the trophy to Tannadice. For ex-chairman Ernest Robertson the wait had been some 54 years but well worth it.[3] And for Aberdeen there was consolation when they won their first Premier League championship in 1980. The New Firm had arrived.

At Dens, however, there was gloom and despondency; Ian Redford was transferred to Rangers for £200,000 and Tommy Gemmell went the way of so many football managers. The club was facing real financial difficulty now but as usual there was no shortage of applicants for the manager's job and this time it went to the amiable Donald McKay, the ex-United goalkeeper. At least McKay had some knowledge of organisation, having worked in England and Europe, and with coach Frank Upton installed as his assistant, the key word became "discipline".

Dundee United Directors and players with the Scottish League Cup 1979. Pictured in Front are: (left to right) Jim McLean (Manager), George Fox (Director), Lord Provost Harry Vaughan, Johnstone Grant (Chairman), Ernest Robertson (Director), Jimmy Littlejohn (Director), George Grant (Director).

(Courtesy: DC Thomson)

The youth policy was overhauled and Ian Ferguson, Stuart McKimmie and Ray Stephen began to challenge for first team places; Cammy Fraser (the same Cameron Fraser whom McLean had signed then released as a sixteen-year-old) was signed from Hearts for £60,000; and against all expectations Dundee FC made it to the 1980-81 League Cup Final, beating Aberdeen over two legs in the semi. What would make this an even more special event, however, was that their opponents would be the holders, Dundee United, and the venue on the toss of a coin, Dens Park.

On Saturday 6 December 1980 the teams lined up. Dundee FC: R Geddes; Barr, Schaedler, Fraser, Glennie, McGeachie, Mackie, Stephen, Sinclair, Williamson and A Geddes. United: McAlpine; Holt, Kopel, Phillip, Hegarty, Narey, Bannon, Payne, Pettigrew, Sturrock and Dodds.

On a cold day, the first-half was evenly contested. Sturrock, however, did not receive the close attention he now required and just before half-time Dodds got on the end of one of his probing crosses to score. In the second-half Dundee had a reasonable penalty claim turned down when McAlpine dived at the feet of Stephen but it did not matter

135

in the final analysis because two late goals from Sturrock sealed Dundee's fate. The (restricted) attendance was 24,700.

Chairman Johnston Grant must have been very proud but, remembering the dark, downtrodden days, he might have been excused for shaking his head when he learned that McLean now had to *ask* the civic authorities if the players could display the cup in the City Square, for no invitation had been forthcoming. The council claimed "a slight hiccup in communications" but I'm sure the old conspiracy was suspected at Tannadice . . .

In Europe United went out again to Lokeren of Belgium on the away goals rule but McLean was not too downhearted. "I feel we are now on the right road to success," he said, and no wonder. Besides his Cup-winning players he had the prospect of still more brilliant youngsters to look forward to. Ralph Milne, for example, a winger whose speed and power promised great things (he had already scored a great goal at Parkhead); Richard Gough, a South African defender, recommended to the club by ex-Dundee stalwart Alec Hamilton; and Maurice Malpas, a cultured and intelligent left-side player.

In the United States events took something of a crazy turn when first John Lennon was shot dead by an obsessed maniac, and then the new President Ronald Reagan was wounded by another individual with the same obsession.

In Dundee, thankfully, things were slightly less crazy. Following on his League Cup achievement MacKay brought the team back up in one season; Paul Sturrock, described by McLean as "the country's most exciting player", was one of Scotland's top goalscorers, capped, and Player of the Year; and United reached the Final of the Scottish Cup (1981) although they lost 4-1 to Rangers in a replay. United: McAlpine; Holt, Kopel, Phillip, Hegarty, Narey, Bannon, Milne, Kirkwood, Sturrock and Dodds. Subs: Pettigrew and Stark.

The club had arrived as a major force in Scottish Football but although even greater things might be ahead of them on paper, no football fan whether connected or unconnected with the club will forget their performances in season 1981-82 and the European games in particular. As League Cup-holders, United once again qualified for the UEFA Cup and in the first round they drew the French club, AS Monaco. Now, as the name suggests, this team came from that famous principality and indeed enjoyed the partonage of Prince

Rainier and Princess Grace (Grace Kelly, the former film star).

> *I remember the time it was an evening game*
> *A European tie in the howlin' rain.*
> *Gus Foye pointed to the side of the goal and said*
> *"There's Grace Kelly by Taylor Brothers Coal"*
> *At Tannadice . . .*
>
> > *–Hamish the Goalkeeper*
> > by Michael Marra.

The first leg was played away and all of Europe got what the French daily newspaper *Nice Matin* described as a "surprise" when the Terrors ran up a 5-2 score. "We did not think," it continued, "that AS Monaco could be beaten so emphatically by *anyone*." However, there were no hard feelings and as it tied in with the marriage of some of their aristocratic chums in Scotland, the return match at Tannadice was witnessed by the Royals themselves. This attracted a number of people who would not normally go to Tannadice and when the home team lost 3-2, McLean was particularly displeased and fined his players. In a way it was understandable for Mrs Thatcher's monetarist economic policies were deliberately creating unemployment (the UK figure was now 3,000,000) and money was scarce.

The team had an early opportunity to restore themselves in the second round when they drew the famous German side, Borussia Münchengladbach. In the first (away) game the score was 2-0 for Borussia but the following Wednesday United scored a brilliant 3-0 victory in the League Cup semi-final against Aberdeen and so by the time the European return game came along the United players were ready to make up for their earlier misdemeanours. In a performance of breathtaking quality they scored no less than five times without a reply and with a rare flash of humour McLean described it as "nothing short of not bad"! Nine of the victorious team had been reared by the club and the other two (Bannon and Hegarty) cost only £200,000. United: McAlpine; Holt, Murray, Gough, Hegarty, Narey, Bannon, Milne, Kirkwood, Sturrock and Dodds.

In the League Cup Final — United's third in succession — Stark replaced Murray and Phillip replaced Gough, and their opponents were Rangers. Milne scored in forty-nine minutes and three minutes

137

later it looked all over when Sturrock crashed in a brilliant thirty-five-yard drive. Holt, however, was adjudged to have been offside and the loss of two goals in the last fourteen minutes meant the Cup was leaving Tannadice.

In Europe, though, they marched on, beating Winterslag of Belgium (0-0 away; 5-0 home). In the quarter-final they were drawn against Radnicki Nis of Yugoslavia. At Tannadice in March 1982 United won 2-0 but in the return the Terrors "froze" and went out 3-0 to what McLean rightly described as "the worst team we have met in competition so far".

NOTES

1 — Former Arsenal star Charlie George also "looked in" at Tannadice in 1982 but failed to make the first team.

2 — Ian Phillip had moved from Dens to Tannadice.

3 — Ernest Robertson died January 1982.

20

DUNDEE FOOTBALL CLUB finished eighth out of ten in season 1981-82 so Donald MacKay had done well in keeping them up, but the financial crisis would not go away and at an Extraordinary General Meeting of the club on 16 March 1982 their debt was so heavy they decided to "go public" in an attempt to raise some capital. 430,000 ordinary shares of £1 were put on the market to be sold in blocks of 250 and the initiative raised £115,000 from public subscription. This compared with a trading loss of £297,000 for one year (ended 31 May 1982) and could only have made a small impression upon the overall debt which was estimated by the press at around £500,000.

The modern Dundee Football Company like the modern Dundee United Football Company and, indeed like a large number of British companies, had its origin during the Second World War. The pre-war company with James A Galloway as Chairman, David How as Vice Chairman and William McIntosh still a major shareholder (Simpson retired in 1939, Galloway in 1944) went into mothballs in 1940 as the previous season's accounts had shown a loss of £1,400 and there were no prospects of the situation improving.

In 1944 "Wattie" Simpson sold 500 shares to James Gellatly and another director, Joseph Murray Wilkie, who was the solicitor appointed to sell the shares of Mr How (now deceased), distributed those in the following manner: 200 to himself on behalf of Mrs How; 490 to James R Gellatly (CA); 900 to James Swadel (cooked meat manufacturer); 900 to Bailie John Thomson and 50 to A P McGill. Swadel and Thomson then sold 400 each to club managing director, George Anderson; Gellatly sold his 490 to Anderson and when

Andrew Clark joined the board in place of Galloway in 1945 it was constituted as follows: Bailie Thomson (Chairman), James R Gellatly, J Swadel, F Graham, A Clark, J M Wilkie and G Anderson, with R Crichton as Company Secretary. Gellatly's firm of accountants took over the audit. Although the players and ex-players of Dundee FC and Dundee United continued to "to and fro" between the clubs, therefore, the business at least was beginning to separate again and this process was completed on the death of William McIntosh in 1955.

McIntosh was something of a king-maker for just as his shares in the United Company gave George Fox and Johnston Grant a firm foothold on the United board, so the distribution of his shares in the Dundee FC Company helped found the dynasty which was to control Dundee Football Club. Gellatly, Clark, Graham and Swadel each received 223 with 148 going to Robert Crichton and when George Anderson died in 1956, the distribution of his shares confirmed the trend (Gellatly 520, Clark 255, Graham 255, Swadel 255).[1]

By the late fifties, therefore, James Gellatly with 1,958 shares was the principal shareholder in Dundee Football Club (other major shareholders were Graham 1,088, Thomson 1,513, Swadel 1,513 and Clark 900). By 1963, having guided them to a League Championship, two League Cups, a Scottish Cup Final and a European Cup semi-final, he was the most successful chairman in the history of the club and one of the most successful provincial chairmen in the history of Scottish Football. By that time, however, he also held nineteen other directorships including one of Reform Properties[2] to which he transferred 1,600 shares in 1962, and had lost out to Dundee United in a crucial initiative in the city, namely, club football pools. This would be one of the factors which would eventually tip the footballing scales in Dundee.

Taypools was begun in 1956 under the Pools Betting Act of 1954. It was run privately by the Dundee United Sportsmen's Club with the proceeds going to the football club.[3] As has been stated earlier, when Johnston Grant and George Fox joined the United board in 1955 under the chairmanship of Ernest Robertson, the club was £10,000 in debt. By 1957 the proceeds of Taypools were responsible for the club going into profit and by 1959 they were worth more than £10,000 annually to Dundee United. This meant the difference between profit and loss, development and stagnation. It meant that the club, properly managed, could now slowly build success on the field.

Dundee FC meanwhile had success — colossal success — which between 1959 and 1966 brought in a net quarter of a million pounds in transfer fees alone, a sum of money which should have enabled them to mount a sustained and effective challenge for honours in Scotland and Europe. But it didn't. It did not even establish a scouting system capable of attracting the cream of young Scottish talent, and in the case of Gordon Strachan in the seventies, even when it did find talent, the club appeared to lose the ability to transfer players at a sensible price. What went wrong?

To my mind it was simply a question of style. Whereas Jim McLean would demonstrate that one man with his feet on the ground, by sheer hard graft and the imposition of simple disciplines in respect of coaching, training and scouting, could build a side of European quality from moderate financial resources, Dundee FC, who had the same man in their employ and let him go to their rivals, seemed to prefer big "names" as managers and big business in the boardroom, when the size of the operation simply did not justify it. Further, companies were not required to disclose dividends paid to directors until 1968. In that year (and this was a few years after the "good times"), from a profit of £11,961.16s.5d, Dundee FC paid a dividend of 25%. In my view this is an extraordinarily high figure when something like 10% is the norm, and probably less in the case of football clubs. By then, housebuilding magnate John Bett had become a Dundee FC director and frankly, with Reform Properties also a major shareholder, the board looked more like that of an estate agent than a football club. Symbolically, James R Gellatly now moved house to the grounds of "Castleroy" — the former baronial home of the jute-owning Gilroy family in Broughty Ferry. Losses of £28,225 and £32,441 were sustained by Dundee Football Club in 1969 and 1971 respectively with a small profit of £720 in 1970. In 1971 Mr I Gellatly (CA), son of James Gellatly, became a director and Company Secretary and 1972 and 1973 were both profitable years (£46,178 and £55,003). In a year which saw no substantial outgoing transfers, however, such as 1974, the difficulties under which Dundee FC were trading were there for all to see. That year the loss was £93,436 and another increase in the share capital looked inevitable. In 1977 with Ian Gellatly installed as chairman, by the creation of 60,000 £1 shares the share capital of the club became £70,000, and of the 70,000 shares the more substantial holdings of directors and their families, and others, were Ian Gellatly (25,356), Ian Bett (3,500),

Albert Bett (3,000),[4] Graham Thomson (5,507) and William Lyburn (5,507). These people were at least putting their money where their mouths were but once again, when one considers the shares held by Reform Properties (12,392)[2] and Inverblair (5,000) the impression of businessmen locked in a game of Monopoly rather than football, persists. And they did not appear to be winning that game either, for losses continued unabated: 1976 (£5,468); 1977 (£56,458); 1978 (£47,682); 1979 (£55,456). One bright spot was that the Dundee FC Sportsmen's Club was now managing to contribute more substantial sums of money (£14,000 in 1976; £28,000 in 1977; £26,000 in 1978), but Taypools by comparison were handing over sums of around £50,000 in these years.

Ironically, whilst Dundee FC headed inexorably towards a public quotation, Dundee United decided to change *their* Articles of Association and become a private company (1972) in which shares could no longer be sold among private individuals but had to be offered first to the directors of the club. Given the experience of Dundee FC in this area, I am not certain of the wisdom of such a move, but at least their policy of promoting ex-players to the board was maintained and first Jim McLean then Doug Smith received directorships in the early 1980s.[5]

In 1982, a life-long fan, Andrew Marshall, a caravan park operator from Cupar, became a director of Dundee FC by virtue of a £25,000 investment; Dundee FC became agents for Rangers Pools; and Bob Shankly and Billy Steel died in the same week.

NOTES

1 — McIntosh's shares were distributed this way as they had to be offered to the board first. More significant, however, was the distribution of the shares of the "Jute Barons" — Simpson, How, Galloway and Graham. It was therefore Jute money which bought power in the club.

2 — Directors (1981) Ronald Gellatly, Ian Gellatly and Jas A Gellatly.

3 — Ernest Robertson originally loaned the money to finance Taypools.

4 — John Bett died 1974. Neither I Bett nor A Bett was a director in 1977. Jas A Gellatly died 1978.

5 — Leading Dundee United shareholders (1983) were: George Fox (2,060), Johnston Grant (2,060), George Grant (1,630) and J McConnachie (1,500). J McLean held 997, J Littlejohn 200 and D Smith 97.

21

UNITED BEGAN season 1982-83 with the signing of Dundonian Ian Britton, a forward who had enjoyed success with Chelsea, and the club was quoted as fourth favourite for the Premier League, at 12-1. In the UEFA Cup they met the crack Dutch side PSV Eindhoven and in the first game at Tannadice the score was 1-1. Once again an intermediate result against Aberdeen (this time 3-1 in the League Cup quarter-final) provided a tonic and the away European game was then won magnificently by 2-0.

Hamish McAlpine was capped as an over age player by the Scottish Under-21 team and in the second round of the UEFA Cup he and his mates outclassed Viking of Stavanger in Norway (3-1 away; 0-0 home). In the third round the German team Werder Bremen was beaten 2-1 at Tannadice and United survived a terrible pounding away from home to secure a 3-2 aggregate win, but with Aberdeen also going well in the Cup Winners' Cup it was generally felt that one or both might land a trophy that year.

In the event it was Ferguson's Dons who did, beating Bayern Munich in the semi-final and Real Madrid in the final, for United were to go out again in the quarter-finals of their tournament, to Bohemians of Prague. They managed to get a good result in Czechoslovakia, going down 1-0, but at Tannadice their goalscoring flair deserted them, so a European semi-final remained a dream. In the League, however, their creative style was pulling in the fans from all over the country and by New Year 1983 they were in second place to Celtic. The Glasgow side had 27 points from 15 games and United 24 points from 15. Dundee FC, who were enjoying some great performances from Cammy Fraser and Ian Ferguson, were in fifth place. The holiday period was a significant time for all three clubs. United utterly dominated Dundee in the derby match, but then lost to Aberdeen, while the Dark Blues went on to Parkhead and won a point in a game which marked the beginning of a slide for Celtic.

The Timex factory was on strike over 1,900 projected redundancies and Clive Sinclair threatened to take his electronic business elsewhere, but the workforce "sat in", for they had recently seen the Robb Caledon shipbuilding workers put out of a job and they were not about to follow suit. In the Scottish Cup it took a last-minute goal by Dundee FC to defeat Brora Rangers at Dens and United went out 1-0 away to St Mirren, but their neighbours had gone down in the Cup to the Buddies and by the same margin, in their championship year, so perhaps this was an omen. Again, Kilmarnock felt the Terrors' wrath, going down heavily for the second time that season, and with Maurice Malpas now a "regular" alongside Gough, the team looked to have a better balance as time went on. Dundee FC were again defeated at Tannadice and although the Bohemians' result came as a blow to McLean his remarks suggested that he still felt as though United could win the League. Again it was a result at Pittodrie which provided the boost when two Ralph Milne goals caught Bayern's conquerors on the hop and again Dundee did them a good turn by beating Celtic 2-1 at Dens.

The positions were now as follows: Aberdeen played 27, points 42; United played 27, points 41; Celtic played 26, points 41; so the League was wide open, but United still had to visit Parkhead twice and the first (Wednesday) game was won 2-0 by Celtic. By now, however, United had five players in the Scotland squad as well as the assistant manager, so confidence was not the problem it had been in previous decades and when the second Celtic match came along on Wednesday 20 April 1983 they were able to put the first result behind them for what was a virtual League decider, given that Aberdeen had also lost points.

The atmosphere at Parkhead was electric and United twice took the lead through Hegarty and Bannon (penalty). Twice they were pulled back, however, and when Gough was ordered off in 58 minutes for becoming unnecessarily involved with Provan, it looked as though their chance had gone. It was at this point that Ralph Milne took a hand in things. Late in the game he controlled a cross from the right and coolly lobbed it over Bonnar in the Celtic goal. "Now you're gonna believe us," sang the United contingent, "We're gonna win the

Dundee United FC Scottish League Champions 1982/83.
Back Row: Dodds, Taylor, Clark, McAlpine, Holt, Narey, Gough, Stark.
Front Row: Milne, Hegarty, Kirkwood, Malpas, Bannon,
(Sturrock missed this game through injury).

(Courtesy: DC Thomson)

League". The Celtic support laughed, like a boxer who had taken a good punch but wanted to unnerve his opponent. The points, however, went to United.

With four games remaining, the Tangerines had to play Kilmarnock (home), Morton (away), Motherwell (home) and Dundee (away). Celtic still had a one point advantage at this stage but Aberdeen who were equal on points beat them (Celtic) 1-0 in the next game. United, meanwhile, beat Kilmarnock 4-0 and in order to take full advantage of their pole position the board hit on an ingenious scheme to give free admission vouchers to fans travelling to Greenock for the Morton game, thereby ensuring a large support. McAlpine had to go off injured in this game but Hegarty was a more-than-capable deputy and United won 4-0.

Aberdeen, still equal on points with United, beat Dundee at Dens but then dropped a point to Hibs, so when United beat Motherwell 4-0

145

in the penultimate game, the City of Dundee was set for a spectacular League decider on Saturday 12 May 1983. Dundee FC *v* Dundee United. Once again the Soap Opera scriptwriter[1] could not have dreamed up a better finale and at least Dundee FC were out of relegation trouble (they finished sixth)..Dundee FC lined up:Kelly, Glennie, McKimmie, Fraser, Smith, MacDonald, Ferguson, McGeachie, Sinclair, Stephen, and Kidd. Subs: Mackie, Scrymgeour. The Dundee United team was: McAlpine, Stark, Malpas, Gough, Narey, Hegarty, Bannon, Milne, Kirkwood, Sturrock and Dodds. Subs: Holt, Reilly.

In the opening minutes, when a gifted player will often try something extraordinary, Ralph Milne picked up a ball in the middle of the Dundee FC half and seeing Kelly off his line, produced a chip goal from nothing. Kelly later made amends by saving a Bannon penalty but the ex-Hearts and Chelsea player followed up to score and although Ferguson pulled one back in 25 minutes, 2-1 was United's League winning margin.[2]

Although the club had used fifteen players in the course of the season, it was a basic twelve players — the winning team, plus Holt — who carried the burden and McLean was quick to point this out during the post-match reception. He was, however, "over the moon" and with St Johnstone winning the First Division and Brechin City the Second, Tayside was Scotland's Champion Region.

NOTES

1 — James A Michener, the popular American author of *Centennial* received part of his education at St Andrews University in the early 1930s. In his book *On Sport* he reveals that during that time he was "a most loyal partisan of Dundee United, in those days the nothing team of the League".

2 — Dundee United's League record for 1982-83 was: played 36, won 24, lost 4, drawn 8, for 90 goals, against 35 goals, points 56.

22

THE PREMIER LEAGUE flag was unfurled at Tannadice on a sunny 20 August 1983, although no TV cameras were there to record the event, owing to an industrial dispute. United demolished Motherwell in the game which followed and Jock Wallace, who had returned from Leicester City to the Lanarkshire club, was fulsome in his praise of their performance. Celtic meanwhile had transferred Charlie Nicholas to Arsenal in the close season and were rumoured to be interested in Paul Sturrock, but the United man was injured in any case and the absence of these two strikers gave Aberdeen something of a head start in the League.

Gordon Wallace left Raith Rovers to take up a coaching position at Tannadice and Dodds was capped against Uruguay, but things remained fairly low-key for the club until Hamrun of Malta were despatched in the first round of the European Cup (3-0 away; 3-0 home). In the second round United faced the Belgian champions Standard Liege and, considering they were still without Sturrock, got a fine 0-0 result away from home in the first leg. Instead of being held up as an example of a fine footballing side, however, United (and every other Scottish club) were relegated to small print by the Scottish press as Rangers went through yet another managerial trauma.

This time John Greig was for the axe — Greig had succeeded Jock Wallace in 1978 — and Alex Ferguson, who was the Ibrox board's first choice to replace him, turned the job down. The diversion suited McLean in a way as he was quietly tuning his players up for the return game with Standard and once again they responded with a magnificent 4-0 home victory. "Bring on Liverpool," chanted the fans and it was

147

known that McLean did indeed fancy a shot at the English champs, but suddenly it was the turn of the United fans to suffer trauma when it was learned that Rangers had now decided McLean was the man they wanted as manager.

In spite of the fact that a reported £65,000 salary was on offer, plus perks and a free hand to sign anyone he wanted — irrespective of religion — it was with disbelief that the United support watched their hero visit Ibrox for talks with the Rangers chairman. Disbelief soon turned to joy, however, for after some deliberation, McLean decided against moving and to stay with United. "No one," said Patrick Barclay of the *Guardian*, "could accuse Rangers of being trendy," but at least they suited Jock Wallace, who now returned to his old stamping ground.

Ironically, on the Saturday before the talks (5 November 1983), a Peter Mackie goal had given Donald McKay his first victory over United since he became manager and for the first time in quite a while Dundee FC seemed to be making progress. There was even talk of Europe again. The irony lay in the fact that one month later it was not McLean but McKay who was on the move, resigning when the club accepted a £90,000 offer for Stuart McKimmie from Aberdeen and failed to buy replacements. His successor was Archie Knox, a man who had been McLean's first "real" signing at Tannadice and until now assistant to Alex Ferguson at Pittodrie. Was he the man to change Dundee's fortunes? Many people in the game certainly thought so.

Meanwhile, back at Tannadice, United had paid £60,000 for one of Clydebank's young strikers, Tommy Coyne; the club was drawn against Rapid Vienna in the quarter-final of the European Cup; and Paul Sturrock pulled a shoulder muscle tying a shoelace! It was not to be his year for fitness. His team-mates were doing reasonably well in the League, however (third; Dundee FC eighth) and in the League Cup, in the semi-final of which they now met Rangers. The tournament had not been much of a success that year — the *Glasgow Herald* suggested sponsorship might come from the Samaritans — and it further soured for United when, following a home draw, McLean got himself into trouble with the SFA for suggesting that too many of his team's games were being handled by West coast officials. Be that as it may, Rangers won the second leg 2-0.

The real stuff was in Europe, however, and in the first (away) game against Rapid, Derek Stark scored a vital goal in 30 minutes. United

*(above) The Dream is over .. Pruzzo (Roma) scores the second goal against
United in Rome (1984).*

(Courtesy: Associated Press Wire Photo)

*(below) Barison (AC Milan) scores the fourth goal against
Dundoo in Milan (1963).*

(Courtesy: Associated Press Wire Photo)

unfortunately lost two late goals but McLean personally thought it was the finest performance he had ever seen from Hamish McAlpine and believed the result to be good enough. The Rapid coach Otto Barie did not agree, claiming that the Austrians would go through as they were "streets ahead" of United but, as Paul Sturrock remarked, the last man to say that was the Borussia coach. It was Sturrock's judgement which proved to be correct.

Archie Knox had a rather indifferent start at Dens but his team performed well in the Scottish Cup and never better than in the quarter-final against Rangers. The first game ended in controversy when a "good" score by Walker McCall[1] was chalked off and it took a brilliant late strike from Albert Kidd[1] to secure a replay.

In the return at Ibrox, Fraser and Ferguson in particular struck a fine game and Dundee beat the 'Gers 3-2. In time-honoured fashion Rangers then signed these two players at the end of the season (1984), thus leaving Knox with something of an uphill struggle, but in any event Dundee FC went out to Aberdeen in the Scottish Cup semi-final and escaped relegation, finishing in eighth place. Knox was quoted as saying that it would take him eight years to put things right at Dens Park.

Before the return match with Rapid Vienna McLean reminded his players of how they had been written-off by the Austrian coach and the ploy worked, for in 21 minutes, Stark mishit a Gough cross and Dodds first-timed the ball into the net with a left-foot shot on the turn. This was enough to give United victory on the away goals rule.

The semi-final of the 1983-84 European Cup was contested by Liverpool, AS Roma, Dinamo Bucharest and Dundee United — again something which speaks for itself — and United drew the Romans with the first game at home.[2] Now, the final was also to be played in Roma's stadium so McLean felt that the draw improved his team's chances of actually winning the competition. But his opinion was not shared by the "intellectual" football correspondent of the *Sunday Times*. In what was probably the first article he had ever written about Dundee United — indeed, it was probably the first time he had ever *thought* about Dundee United — the supercilious Brian Glanville dismissed them as a "biff-and-bang" side whose tactics would not trouble Roma. How anyone could describe a team which contained Maurice Malpas, David Narey, Eamonn Bannon, Ralph Milne and Paul Sturrock as playing "up-and-at-em" football is a mystery but

Glanville noticably gave the subject a body swerve on Sunday 15 April for by then United were ahead by two goals to nil.

Roma, of course, were a great side. Coached by Nils Liedholm who, strangely enough, had also worked for AC Milan in 1963, they were a rich club who had spent their money on some brilliant players like Brazilian Roberto Falcao and the Italian World Cup star, Bruno Conti. Falcao in particular was the man who made the team tick and when he missed the first leg at Tannadice through injury, United took full advantage, scoring through Dodds in 48 minutes and Stark in 60. Almost unbelievably, United could have had more, for that twelve-minute spell shook the Italians' confidence and both Milne and Hegarty came near. The game finished 2-0, however, and again McLean thought it was enough.

In the League he was not deriving the same satisfaction, for in a game against Dundee FC he again clashed with referee Alan Ferguson and, following the Roma match, Aberdeen ended his championship hopes for that year. The former incident was to have particularly unpleasant personal consequences for the United manager because, later in the season, he was fined by the SFA and banned from the touchline for a year, a decision which would cost him his assistant managership of the Scotland team.

In Rome it was death or glory. The return game was played in the suitably gladiatorial Olympic Stadium and watched by 68,060 people who paid £600,000 for the privilege — a record for an Italian club match. United lined up: McAlpine, Stark, Malpas, Gough, Hegarty, Narey, Bannon, Milne, Kirkwood, Sturrock and Dodds. The game kicked off at 3 pm and at two minutes past three United were given formal notice of the task in hand when Conti put the ball in the net. The "goal" was chalked off but this was the point of no return for United. Gamely they tried to take the match to Roma and in 20 minutes almost scored when Dodds' brave dive for a Bannon cross gave Milne a chance. He steadied in front of the open goal but the shot went over the bar and that, as they say, was that. Pruzzo scored in 21 minutes with a header and in 38 minutes with a shot, and in the second half a Di Bartolomi penalty ended United's dream. Everyone — including McLean who was shamefully harassed by the Italian players at the end — admitted that the better side had won, but it once more fell to Glanville to scrape the bottom of the barrel. "Poor, limp, mediocre Dundee United" was one description and "naive" another.

Well, by Italian, English or even Scottish standards United are not a rich club. The players certainly did not give one of their best performances in Rome. But for a football club to come from the bottom four of the Scottish Second Division to the top four of Europe; from a wee, wooden stand built before the First World War, to the Olympic Stadium in Rome; to do this in 25 years, breaking, as they did, the century-old domination of Scottish football by the Old Firm along the way — the achievements of Dundee United in my opinion are without parallel in club football.

One more thing. Brian Glanville also described them in a kind of literary joke as "plebians". Little did he know that in so doing he was fulfilling the stated ambition of one of the founding fathers of Dundee United Football Club, namely, to make them "the people's club".[3]

NOTES

1 — McCall was a former Ayr United and Aberdeen player who had come to Dundee via Hong Kong. Albert Kidd, a Dundonian, cost McKay a record £80,000 when he was transferred from Motherwell.

2 — The home game, to the month, celebrated United's seventy-fifth Anniversary — or to be more accurate — it was seventy-five years since the birth of Dundee Hibs.

3 — Johnston Grant died in July 1984. He was widely regarded as the "father" of the modern Dundee United.

23

ALTHOUGH I WAS aware even as a child in the fifties that Dundee United were a poorer club financially than Dundee FC, it was much later that I heard United described as the "working-man's team", the inference being that Dundee FC somehow are not. Now this to anyone who has seen the broad composition of the Dark Blue support is plainly nonsense for the vast majority of their fans come from the working classes and are indistinguishable from those of United, yet the idea persists that Dundee FC consider themselves to be a better "class" of club than United who apparently must remain the poor relations in spite of their superior results and financial performance over the last ten years. United have equalled Dundee in every respect (except the winning of the Scottish Cup, and Dundee's success was seventy-five years ago) yet when they (United) were invited to a nationally-sponsored exhibition of Scottish football memorabilia in Dundee in 1983, their invitation came on the back of a facsimile of a cigarette card depicting a Dundee FC player. Is it any wonder they declined or that their mild, media paranoia intensified?

How did such attitudes arise? If we look at the historical facts we find that although Dundee FC are technically the older club, it can be argued that Tannadice Park is the older ground, football having been played on Clepington Park some twenty years before a ball was kicked at Dens, and since the principal forebears of both clubs, Our Boys and Harp, saw the light of day at approximately the same time it is perhaps the superior playing record of Harp in the 1880s upon which attention should be focused rather than the grand delusions of Our Boys who apparently looked down their noses even at their partners, East End.

153

It was the Dundee FC amalgamation, however, which seized the commercial initiative and from the 1890s onwards there is no doubt that the Dark Blues were the "big" Dundee club. For the next thirty years professional football in the city and Dundee Football Club were synonymous. There is also no doubt however that the body of men who founded Dundee FC in 1893 and rebuilt it at the turn of the century were ordinary working people — and the same was true of Pat Reilly's Dundee Hibs.

The clubs appear to have been closest in terms of their status, support and ambitions in 1925 when the re-constituted Hibs, Dundee United, prepared to enter the First Division. This was a time of great hope at Tannadice and had things gone according to plan they would soon have had a stadium to match the new Dens Park and a team to do it justice. But it was not to be. Of course, in the midst of the social turmoil of the time, even the well-laid plans of William McIntosh, that pillar of the Dundee Football Club establishment, went slightly aglae and the complexity of the new situation as it developed over the *next* thirty years is perhaps best exemplified by the career of the Dundee FC and SFA treasurer. McIntosh was a hard-working and popular official both with the players and the fans who could readily give him a piece of their mind over the counter at the Opera Bar. He badly overstepped himself by opposing the advancement of Hibs and even their choice of name thus causing a great deal of ill-feeling amongst the Hibs' fans whose Irish ancestry had taught them a great deal about the misuse of power, and yet ironically it was McIntosh himself who, ten years later, was to feel the Iron Heel. For although Dundee FC had a grand new stadium, it still had to be paid for, and if the club was not enjoying success on the park their money would have to be found from a source other than their supporters. And where was there money in Dundee? In Jute. Or to be more precise in the hands of a small number of "jute barons", mill owners, merchants and the like.

McIntosh now proceeded to encourage a number of them, Simpson, How, Galloway and Graham, to involve themselves in the affairs of Dundee Football Club and, looking upon it as just another business investment they responded in the only way such people know how — by climbing to power then kicking the ladder away. Willie McIntosh was duly forced out and how poetic it was that the main beneficiaries of Dundee FC's most crucial power struggle should be their greatest rivals, Dundee United. For at the bottom line, it was *football* which really interested McIntosh and, having swallowed his pride and crossed the road: (i) his administrative experience would have been invaluable to a small club with a cash crisis of its own; and (ii) his bitter experience at Dens would have given him the resolve to make sure that United did not similarly fall into the clutches of the capitalists. "Ownership means control" and "stay small think big" might have been his guiding principles at Tannadice and this approach has served the club well.

The way things turned out, of course, could not have been better written by James Michener — that *aficionado* of Dundee football himself — for while United re-grouped around a board which included people who actually knew something about football (i.e. ex-players) and consolidated their support amongst the ancestors of immigrant jute *workers,* Dundee FC were stuck with power in the hands of jute *owners* and their appointed heirs. In a sense, *their* fans might have known what to expect and surely, this was the time when the "image" of the Dundee clubs was cast.

Image, however, is not everything and whilst the inevitability of the historical process was never more in evidence than in the professional football arenas of the city of Dundee over the last thirty, or indeed, one hundred years there is always the potential for change *if the lessons of history are learned.* For while United now constitute themselves on a private basis the shares of Dundee FC are once again available to the general public (albeit at a price), so who knows what might happen? The fact that many people *care* suggests that the game, at least, is in good hands. Football is not "just another business". Here's to the next hundred years.

Bibliography

William M Walker. *Juteopolis: Dundee and its Textile Workers 1885-1923.* Scottish Academic Press.

John Cottrell. *A Century of Great Soccer Drama.*

John Ramsden. *The Age of Balfour and Baldwin,* Volume 3 in *The History of the Conservative Party.* Longman.

Jimmy Guthrie. *Soccer Rebel.*

1878/79. *The Scottish Football Annual of the Scottish Football Association.*

J M Jackson, Ed. *The City of Dundee.* The Third Statistical Account of Scotland 1979.

D S Riddell. *Social Structure and Relations.* The Third STatistical Account of Scotland 1977.

D S Riddell. *Leisure (1961).* The Third Statistical Account of Scotland 1977.

k Brasch. *How Did Sports Begin.* Longman.

Tony Mason. *Association Football and English Society 1863-1915.* Stanley Paul.

John Rafferty. *One Hundred Years of Scottish Football.* Pan Books.

B Lenman and K Donaldson. *Partners, Incomes, Investments and Diversification in the Scottish Linen Area.* Business History XIII No 1. (1971) 18.

James Michener. *On Sport.* Secker & Warburg.

John Hutchison. *The Football Industry.* Richard Drew.

Wm McGonagall. *More Poetic Gems.* Duckworth.

H B Boyne. *Dark Blue Down the Years.* Simmath Press.

H B Boyne. *Dundee United FC Through the Years.* Simmath Press.

Forrest Robertson, Ed. *Mackinlay's A-Z of Scottish Football.* MacDonald Publishers 1979.

S J Jones, Ed. *Dundee & District.* British Association.

John Prebble. *The High Girders.* Secker & Warburg, 1956.

D Phillips. *Jimmy Shand: A Biography.* Winter.

The following list of periodicals have proved invaluable sources for the research for this book.

Newspapers
The Advertiser
The Courier
The Courier and Advertiser
Daily Record
Dundee Evening Telegraph and Post
Glasgow Herald
The Glasgow Observer
The Guardian
The People's Journal
The Scotsman
Scottish Referee
Scottish Sport
Scottish Umpire
Sport Illustrated
The Sporting Post
Sunday Mail
Sunday Post
The Sunday Standard
The Sunday Times

Others
Dundee and Round About
The Dundee Directory
The Dundee FC Programme
The Dundee United FC Programme
The Dundee United Handbook
Who's Who of Scottish Internationalists